Johann Trollı

and

Romani Resistance to the Nazis

Jud Nirenberg

Win By KO Publications

Iowa City

Johann Trollmann and Romani Resistance to the Nazis

Jud Nirenberg

(ISBN-13): 978-0-9903703-7-6

(softcover: 50# acid-free alkaline paper)

Includes endnotes

© 2016 by Jud Nirenberg. All Rights Reserved.

No part of this book may be reproduced, or transmitted in any form or by any means, graphic, electronic or mechanical, including photocopying, recording, taping, or by any information storage retrieval system without the written permission of Jud Nirenberg.

Cover art and design by Rima Salloum ©.

Manufactured in the United States of America

Win By KO Publications
Iowa City, Iowa
winbykopublications.com

Table of Contents

Thanks	5
Germany's Best	7
Roma, Sinti and the Holocaust: What is in a Word	10
Trollmann's Enduring Relevance	11
The Roma, Sinti and History	14
A Fighter's Roots	24
Boxing Comes Out	31
Lean and Hard Years	38
Rukeli Finds His Style	42
Schmeling vs. Baer	62
Trollmann's Title Shot	65
Survival: 1934-1936	75
The 1936 Olympics	80
Schmeling vs. Louis	88
War Spreads	95
The Pot Boils	107
Resistance in Romania	120
Rukeli in the Camps	126

Protestors, Soldiers and Partisans	137
Aftermath	140
Discrimination and Exclusion After the War	148
The Struggle for Holocaust Memory	157
Where the Genocide is Remembered	203
Race Politics in Sport Today: Andrea Pirlo and Tyson Fury	207
Bokhale Mulenca/Hungry Ghosts, by Qristina Cummings	211
Endnotes	215

Thanks

I thank all those who cooperated in this project; Diana Sima and Tim Olin for helping with translations, writers Hank Rosenfeld and Daniel Kravetz for their eyes and suggestions, and the many people who shared their stories and views such as Dani Karavan, Ethel Brooks, Asmet Elezovski, the Trollmann family, Erich Seelig's son Mac, Jan Yoors' son Kore and the experts at the US Holocaust Memorial Museum who shared their experiences.

I thank my wife, Liz for her encouragement and for sharing my belief in preserving overlooked peoples' history.

I thank Dr. Donald Kenrick, whose work is sourced in these pages, who took me on as an intern when I was a student and who was among the very first writers to study the Romani genocide. Dr. Kenrick passed away in 2015 but his kind efforts on behalf of many Romani immigrants in the UK and his work to preserve Romani history and dialects leave immortal marks.

I thank the Roma and Sinti survivors who knew the importance of telling their stories. The following is offered with great respect to all those whose words and losses are mentioned.

Finally I thank my son, Emmet for his patience when I was writing and he wanted to play.

"*He who wants to live must fight, and he who does not want to fight in this world of perpetual struggle does not deserve to live!*"

-Adolph Hitler, *Mein Kampf*

Germany's Best

The Nazis paid close attention to boxing. It was no normal sport to them, and certainly not to Hitler. Young German men were, he wrote, to practice and to be honed for war by it. They were to be emboldened and inspired by boxing. And so the Nazis ruled that Jews could no longer take part. There were to be no more Jews in boxing as fighters, no trainers, no cut men, no ringside Jewish doctors. Out.

The law was too important to just pass in the Reichstag and then leave to the police. It was enforced with urgency and a personal touch. Erich Seelig, the Jewish national light-heavyweight champion of Germany, whom Hitler had the unsettling experience of watching from a front row seat and whose success made the world's most ardent believer in Aryan superiority so uncomfortable, was sent a letter giving him two weeks to leave both the sport and the country. When his time was up, men were sent to his home. Nestled in the back seat of a car between stern officers with guns to his head, Seelig was given a ride straight to the airport. His family, they told him, would die if he came back.

The national title was open, waiting for a new boxing hero.

The government-controlled sports press made clear who ought to win as Adolf Witt and Johann Trollmann prepared to enter the ring. Witt had to come out on top. Trollmann, who had been mentored by the Jewish Seelig, was no proper example of a German fighting man. He was a racial inferior, a Gypsy. As he was the fighter with the best record in his weight class, there was no getting around letting him fight for the title and yet *Box-Sport* claimed his style had "little to do with boxing". He danced, he was unpredictable. He was sneaky, they wrote. They claimed he used instincts rather than brains. He liked "jumping around" too much before knocking his opponents out. He was an insult to brave white men.

It was a month after the nationwide burning of un-German books when Trollmann and Witt entered the ring at Berlin's enormous Bockbierbraurei beer hall. It was an open air ring and a storm was coming. Fans pulled their homburgs down and leaned forward in wooden seats.

Witt won the first round before Trollmann figured him out. From there, it was no competition. Trollmann scored repeatedly with his left. Witt tried to go for solid blows but found the Gypsy's footwork too elusive.

It was intolerable. The devoted Nazi and head of the national boxing association, Georg Radamm ran to the ring and whispered to the referee, who could find no grounds to stop the fight or influence the results. Only the boxers could determine who would win.

The bell sounded at the end of the twelfth and final round. The crowd waited. "No decision," called out the referee. The title stayed open. For the longest time there was no sound or movement.

And then the crowd awoke, went mad, shouting and leaping from their seats. Trollmann's manager followed the mood. He cursed. He ran around the ring and made threats. He grabbed the judges' scorecards and showed them to anyone who would look. Trollmann had clearly won by all judges' counts. Fights broke out in the stands. Radamm and the promoters came to stand together before the audience and called for order. They would take a look at the scorecards. They made a show of examining the cards. Yes, there had been an error.

Trollmann was declared the winner and the new light-heavyweight champion. A man of a dark-skinned race that government policy had determined unclean and a danger to Aryan society had risen to become Germany's top athlete in a sport that Hitler and Nazism had deemed as the best demonstration of courage and warrior spirit. The public cheered him.

On Monday, the boxing association's leaders met and quickly nullified the result. The title would be registered as having no decision as a result of "the insufficient effort of both fighters". It was also alleged that Trollmann was not worthy of the title because he had been unsportsmanlike and cried (after the announcement of the no decision).

When Trollmann next fought a month later, he had dropped to a lower weight class to fight against Dortmund's Gustav "Eisener" (*Iron*) Eder.

Eder was shorter and lighter, even after Trollmann's rapid weight loss. Did it matter what weight class he was in, or how he performed? Had it not been proven that the white man, the German man would always win? He had to.

As the crowds cheered for the show to begin, Trollmann came down the aisle toward the ring. He was unrecognizable. His hair was dyed a nearly white blond. Shiny and wet, he was covered from head to calves in some sort of white powder. Is this what they wanted? Would he have to change color to be a real German?

He did more than change his look that night. It was no longer about winning. He fought as the commentators had said an Aryan should. From the first round, he kept his feet rooted to the canvass. He dared Eder to come toe to toe, with no retreat. He challenged the public and the boxing press to face their racial obsession.

Trollmann fought on. While the fascist regime rounded up Sinti and Roma, or "Gypsies" for deportation to the concentration camps, he fought for his country – fought for Nazism – on the front lines in France and the Soviet Union. While he fought for Germany, many other Roma and Sinti fought against it, in their countries' militaries and in underground resistance groups. In fascist Romania, where the authorities simultaneously deported Roma to die in the snows of Transnistria and conscripted them into the army, Roma in uniform forced the regime to back down from its ethnic cleansing.

The following is the story of how Trollmann and many other Roma and Sinti struggled, resisted, died and survived the Holocaust, how society and governments turned individual athletes, complex human beings into simplistic symbols of racial politics and how the fight for the memory of the Roma and Sinti in the war years goes on.

Roma, Sinti, Gypsies and the Holocaust: What is in a Word

The word *Roma* refers to members of a specific ethnic group. It is the largest ethnic minority in Europe today and by many measures the most socio-economically excluded. *Sinti* are a closely related but distinct ethnic group. Both are called Gypsies by outsiders.

The word *Gypsy* has, depending on the dictionary or the speaker, many definitions and most are in relation to a person's behavior. To call someone a Gypsy is to call him a wanderer, a nomad, a thief, a "cunning or crafty" person (according to Webster's) or a fortune-teller. How can one use the word Gypsy to refer to Roma or Sinti without being guilty of prejudice? One cannot. The word is incorrect. It is used frequently in this text because it was an official classification of innocent people under Nazism and other governments. Roma, Sinti and some other communities were lumped together as constituting a Gypsy race.

Genocide is the systematic elimination of an ethnic, racial, national or religious group and there is no doubt that this is what the Nazis and their collaborators attempted to do to the Roma and Sinti.

The *Holocaust* is often defined as the German genocide of approximately six million Jews. In this book, the word Holocaust is often used to describe Nazi genocide of both Jews and Gypsies, though many scholars oppose any use of the word to cover gentile victims. Today some Romani activists and scholars promote a special term for the Romani genocide, *porrajmos*. This word, however, has its own unfortunate connotations, as it comes from the verb *to force open* or *to rape*. Other Roma prefer *samudaripe*, literally meaning a *murder of all*. For common Romani and Sinti people, there is no term more recognized or understood than Holocaust.

Trollmann's Enduring Relevance

In a way, Johann "Rukeli" Trollmann *is* the Romani and Sinti Holocaust. His brother's granddaughter Diana says, "In Germany, for the Sinti, Rukeli is our Anne Frank." Like Sinti losses in the Holocaust, he is a constant symbol of the past and a warning of the possible among his own people, yet he is largely unknown to most of the world.

His fight resonates. Speaking of Johann Trollmann and his ethnic identity, Sinto and former West German champion boxer Robert Marschall says: "You have to learn how to struggle, to pick yourself up if you fall…Otherwise as a Sinto you are lost from the very start."[1]

This book is not only about Trollmann. The later chapters focus on the effort of some Roma and Sinti today to create awareness of what their people experienced, lost and defended during the Holocaust. While 95% of Americans say they've heard about the Holocaust, a majority of high school students cannot give a definition of the word. Only 21% answered that yes, the Warsaw ghetto has something to do with the Holocaust.[2] The word is connected to popular movies and icons but decoupled from the history of ethnic segregation in Europe or of fascism. If people know little about how and why powerful movements came to attempt – and nearly accomplish – the elimination of Europe's Jews, they know far less about the one other ethnic group that Nazis and their collaborators marked for complete extermination.

When one thinks of genocide or of the Holocaust, one thinks of victims and oppressors. One thinks of heroic liberators and just maybe of those who fought back with more limited resources; the protestors, the underground resistance, the acts of defiance that are so important precisely because they are quixotic. Unlike in the movies, reality does not always give us simple heroes and villains. Fascism lasted much longer than a Hollywood drama. People in its grip had occasion to play many roles. Ethel Brooks notes that we usually "maintain categories of survivor, victim and perpetrator"[3] in looking at the Holocaust. Trollmann and the other Roma and Sinti in this story remind us that people do not fit into neat categories, especially not in the most chaotic of times. Johann Trollmann challenged many strong men in his life. Out of the ring and inside it, he challenged German government and society. In death, he has had victories that eluded him in his lifetime. He challenges our ideas about how members of ostracized minority groups engage with society in times of the most extreme exclusion.

To understand Johann Trollmann's life, we need context. He lived in a society that made ethnic heritage paramount, and so the story must begin with the origins of the Sinti, the "Gypsy" community from which he came. His story also does not end with his death in 1943, since his career in a very real way ended only in 2003, when he was posthumously re-awarded his title as a national champion. Both the fight to preserve the memory of the Roma and Sinti who were murdered in the 1940s and the effort to remember Trollmann specifically continues even today. For decades after the Holocaust, Germans learned that Gypsies were not victims of racial death policy but were targeted because they were "asocial". The libel that the murdered were selected for some kind of improper, asocial behavior took a concerted and long-term struggle to rectify.

To grasp Trollmann's response to racism, we need to do more than imagine how we would have felt in his shoes; we should note how different, how much bolder and more clearly he saw the inhumanity of norms that other athletes of the era took as merely unfortunate facts of life. Trollmann didn't swallow mistreatment. He was a fighter. There is an old Romani saying, *"nashtik djas vorta po bango drom";* we cannot go straight on a crooked path. Trollmann did not always take the anti-fascist stand. He lived within German society and often struggled to be an accepted part of the only world he knew. Yet compared to many other victims of racial bias and violence, he showed unusually consistent awareness of his own humanity and willingness to carry on, to struggle. Others resisted and they too have a place in the story.

He was not only a great boxer, not just a champion in a country that was a world leader in sports. Still, appreciating his boxing is one starting point. A boxer must be an excellent athlete and he was. Others have written that he was, even as a child, a faster runner, stronger swimmer than his peers. To box well, physical prowess is not enough. The sport requires strategic and tactical decision-making, and decisions made quickly. The boxer who wins has to examine his opponent's style and habits, to analyze, to build a hypothesis of how he can be beaten. Then he needs to test the hypothesis, consider the results of the test, and try something new. Boxing, after all, is often called the "sweet science". A successful plan yields insight that can only be used a few times before the strategy becomes predictable, and then the boxer has to start all over. It is a lot of thinking and it has to be done while the body part we use for thinking is beaten and shaken. The strategy must be formed while the boxer struggles for air, runs in a tight circle, experiences sudden pain. It takes detachment from, or transcendence of the self. Trollmann took the light-heavyweight title in Germany. He could transcend.

To understand Johann Trollmann, one should understand that his name was not Johann. That was a name used with outsiders but not in his family or community. It was a name to use when speaking German. At home, where the language of the Sinti was spoken, he was Rukeli, or Little Tree. Though Rukeli was in many ways just like any German child, or at least any German boy of his economic situation at the beginning of the century, he was nonetheless defined, held back and ultimately slaughtered because of this difference, because he was a Sinto. As he reached his athletic peak, Germany pursued a political vision in which racial theories were central and in which boxing held a special symbolic place. To understand the injustice of Trollmann's life, we need to see how greatly the beliefs of the time – as well as many of today's common ideas – about Gypsies and about ethic identity were, and still are so mistaken.

The Roma, Sinti and History

Today Roma are the largest ethnic minority in Europe. Perhaps ten to twelve million Roma live in Europe if one counts all the people of the Romani diaspora, such as the Sinti. Romani children are, in several countries, still mostly placed in segregated and inferior educational settings. In some countries, Roma are put in schools that are officially for the learning disabled but predominantly populated by Roma. Even in many supposedly integrated schools, Roma are put in separate classrooms. Placed in learning environments where little teaching is done, Roma commonly drop out in their teenage years. Job discrimination is common even for those Roma who do have employable skills. While employment discrimination is illegal in most of Europe, enforcement of anti-discrimination laws is not easy. Uneducated, unemployed and disliked, Roma typically live in slums, apart from non-Roma. Richard John Neuhaus, editor of the well-reputed and widely read American publication *First Things* calls Gypsies "lazy, lying, thieving, and extraordinarily filthy people". Otherwise intellectual people voice opinions of Roma that would be quickly rebuked as stupid bigotry if said about any other ethnic community. [4]

While Roma who live in mobile homes or caravans are very visible to the outside world, they are a tiny fraction of the millions of Roma in Europe and the world. While Romani children begging or picking pockets in crowded tourist attractions remind the passersby of some very old and well-known stereotypes, they are, again, a tiny segment of a large community. The great majority of Roma do not steal, beg or live a nomadic lifestyle. Outsiders often look at the beggars and the migrants and suppose that those Roma are living according to an ancient culture. This is not so. There are some Roma and Sinti who see life in a caravan as a family tradition. The travel patterns of the Trollmann family as Rukeli was growing up, discussed in pages ahead, provide an opportunity to separate myth from reality. There are more who move for the reasons Roma have always moved – they are seeking a new life, a way to provide for a family.

Yet it is true that most Roma are poor and live outside of Europe's opportunities and society. How did it come to this?

Much is debated about the history of the Roma. Most likely in the sixth century A.D., the first groups of the Roma's ancestors left northwestern India for the Persian empire. In 1001, when the Islamic leader Mahmud of Ghazni invaded India, another wave of Indians, mostly lower-caste men were conscripted to wage war against the Muslims across northern India and Persia for over three decades of conflict. In a series of waves, Indians found their way into Persia as slaves, as mercenaries, as merchants and more. The first people to call themselves Roma and to speak a language called Romani were in the Persian Empire and had roots in India. Perhaps the Romani identity, then, has always been that of a people in diaspora, a people with roots somewhere else. The Roma would migrate, as did many other people, into Byzantium and, as the Byzantine Empire enlarged, into southeastern Europe. By the 14th century and perhaps earlier, Roma were as far west as Bohemia (in today's Czech Republic). By the 15th century, they were nearly everywhere in Europe, from Russia and the northeast to Scotland, Sweden, Portugal and points in between, including Germany. Crossing borders into new lands, some Roma told authorities that they were penitents from Egypt. They claimed to be former Muslims using pilgrimage to Western holy sites to pay for their heathen past. The myth that Roma came from Egypt is the origin of the English word Gypsy and the Spanish word *gitano*.

Some local nobility in central Europe actively encouraged Roma to settle in their lands, with promises of reasonable taxes and offers of work. Roma were reputed to have highly skilled horse breeders and trainers and metal smiths among their numbers. For dukes or small lords with eastern invaders on their minds, such skills were of the highest value.

If their skills were valued by some, Roma were still from the east, strangers coming from the non-Christian world at a time when Christendom was insecure. They were non-white at a time when Christians were taught that blackened skin was the mark of Cain and of wickedness. It took little time for anti-Romani sentiment to arise. Roma were ordered expelled from the Meissen region (Germany) in 1416. In the 1400s and 1500s rulers across Europe forbade the

Gypsies from entering or settling in their territories. In 1510, a law in Switzerland ordered all Gypsies put to death on sight.

In Wallachia, Transylvania and Moldavia, Roma were enslaved for five centuries, until abolition in the 1860s, very shortly before the end of the enslavement of African-Americans in the United States.

In 1710, Hapsburg ruler Joseph I ordered all adult males hanged without trial and women flogged and banished forever. They were to have their right ears cut off in the kingdom of Bohemia and their left ear in Moravia. Augustus of Saxony, a year later, picked up on the trend and passed law forbidding all Gypsies from coming to his lands. Violators were flogged and branded with hot iron. If they ever came back, they were to be hanged.

Chasing Roma from place to place did not, as one might guess, set the stage for integration. Roma ended up poor, migratory and apart from majorities both economically and culturally. As Europe failed to keep this large population out, policies turned toward how to make them assimilate. In Spain, the Romani language was forbidden and violators' tongues were to be cut out.

In 1758, the Hapsburg ruler and Holy Roman Empress Maria Theresa began a program of assimilation to turn Roma into *ujmagyarok* (new Hungarians). Whether Roma were migrating by choice or in search of lands where they were allowed to live (and where they could make a living), policy determined now to force them from their presumably chosen nomadism. The empire replaced Romani mobile tents and horse-drawn wagons with permanent huts and forcefully removed many children from their parents to be placed in adoptive non-Romani homes. In practice, in many parts of the empire the policy meant taking away the working assets of people who were earning a living as travelling, skilled craftsmen or merchants and making them into impoverished serfs. It forced surviving and independent families who were mobile and difficult to tax to become poor dirt farmers, who were more easily exploited by the nobility. Then again, it must have taken some Roma who wandered without resources and assigned them to land and sharecropping lives. In any case, by 1894, the majority of Roma in a Hungarian national census were sedentary (living in one location).

However Roma lived, they were seen by majorities as different and savage. In 1830 Romani children in Nordhausen (in western Germany, a bit to the south of Hannover) were taken from their families to be fostered by Germans.

The image of the primitive Gypsy who refused work, who refused to settle into the norms of others, fit with the preoccupations of the time. In the 1800s, Romanticism in the arts and literature searched for a "noble savage", for primitive man who resisted the Industrial Revolution and European mores. Many writers and painters cast Roma in this role. Real Romani people's views were not generally sought. When many Roma were emancipated from slavery in southeastern Europe in the 1860s, a new migration wave rekindled the view that Roma were and wished to be nomads. It hardly mattered that these wanderers had lived for centuries on the same estates and that their travel was something new for them.

At the start of the twentieth century, Roma were widely disliked. They were seen as unable or unwilling to fit in. In several countries, including Poland, the Soviet Union, Czechoslovakia and the United States, some Roma set up cultural, charitable and political associations that aimed at improved integration and at challenging discrimination.

There is a piece of folklore that circulates among some Sinti and Roma. Hitler, some say, went to a Romani fortune-teller. Looking into a crystal ball, she promised him great power. She also said that his fall would be more sudden than his rise. He was furious. He decided that he could break the curse of the prediction if he broke the race that issued it. The truth is that we need no special story to understand Hitler's and so much of Europe's belief that the Gypsies should die. The racial dogma the Nazis brought to a logical conclusion was neither a new nor exclusively German concept. If the murder of Sinti and Roma had been a radical and unpleasant idea to everyone, it would not have been so effectively applied. It was not always controversial. In German-occupied Serbia, there was no specific directive from Berlin to exterminate the Roma. Local military commanders just went ahead and did it.

At the beginning of the twentieth century, many members of Germany's small Sinti and Romani communities lived no differently than their non-Gypsy neighbors. When Johann Trollmann's parents married, in 1901, their families had been in northern Germany and the Hannover area for centuries. Seen in comparison to many of Europe's Gypsies, Germany's Sinti were not faring poorly. The majority of them had permanent homes. Those who were "traveling" and who had wagons or caravans – as the Trollmanns *sometimes* used - only really kept such quaint means of travel for business travel or for summer and holiday visits to relatives.

The Wintersteins were another such a family whose fate we will read. They had been property owners for several generations before World War Two. They had a house and barn in a small town called Lohr am Main, on the Main River. The family provided grapes to several wineries. The children all went to school. They did not fit many of the majority's fantasies about Gypsies. This would not matter. In fact, whereas the Nazi slaughter of Jews began with those who Nazi definitions treated as fully Jewish and only later extended to those of mixed background, the Nazi ideas about Gypsies treated those from mixed families – often the most integrated and assimilated ones, to be the most threatening to German society. Gypsies who lived among white neighbors and who intermarried were a danger to racial purity of the German *Volk,* or nation more than those who lived on the road and had limited social contact with whites. Long before Nazis took government and before policies were formulated for the genocide of Jews, the government employed racial hygienists such as Robert Ritter and politicians wrote of the need to eliminate people of mixed (partial) Gypsy heritage through sterilization and concentration or internment in camps.

The idea that Roma and Sinti were genetically prone to crime was not unique to Germany. In Austria, before Germany annexed their neighbor, there was governmental discussion of resettling all Austria's Sinti to islands in the South Pacific.[5] In Italy, leading criminologists such as Cesare Lombroso believed that Roma and Sinti were "the living example of a whole race of criminals".[6]

And yet the Roma and Sinti of Germany did not see the genocide coming. Many Roma and Sinti could not fathom what was happening or why as they were gathered up with no warning, not allowed to take a winter jacket and brought to detention centers, then to the trains that delivered them to the camps. Years after forced incarceration in concentration camps began, many could not imagine what was ahead. Pale from fatigue after sleepless days and nights, already losing weight from lack of food, circles around their eyes and noses running after days in unheated transport, Gypsy men stood proudly in their military uniforms and displayed medals for their combat service to the Fatherland. Surely nobody could doubt that they were honorable and loyal Germans? The gap between how they saw themselves and how the majority viewed them was out of their grasp even as the evidence became nightmarish.

Having considered the Roma, what of the Sinti? Who are they?

In present Germany, discrimination against the Sinti has not disappeared. Surviving members of the Trollmann family have made the fight against discrimination, and not only against Sinti, central to their lives, as we will see in later pages.

While there may be twelve million Roma in Europe, there are probably not more than 80,000 Sinti.[7] Even this estimate seems inflated, as it includes the Manouche of France. While the Manouche are seen by some outsiders as kind of Sinti, most Manouche insist that they are neither Sinti nor Roma[8] and have their own proud identity. Sinti, whatever their current numbers, were before the war and are still the majority of Germany's "Gypsies". Outside of Germany and Austria, one often forgets them when speaking of Roma. In Germany, one does not.

Jud Nirenberg was once asked his ethnic background at a dinner party in Germany. He explained his mixed and included Roma.
"In Germany, we say Roma and Sinti," the German interlocutor corrected.

"Yes, well, I'm only Roma. There are no Sinti in my family."

Taken aback by the failure to use politically correct language, the German lowered his voice and repeated, "*We* say Roma and Sinti." The idea of two distinct ethnicities was lost on him.

The Sinti seem to many observers similar to Roma in appearance, in culture and, of course, in the history of persecution at the hands of outsiders. To many, Roma and Sinti are all Gypsies and the distinctions hardly matter. Yet many Sinti are quick to point out that they are *not* Roma.

In the past, it was widely assumed by anthropologists and others that Sinti are a subgroup of Roma and that the first Sinti were Roma who somehow formed, while living in German-speaking Europe, a sub-identity and unique dialect. The predominant view today is different. It is very likely that the Sinti have always been a distinct people, even if they have always been closely linked to the Roma. Perhaps the Sinti, who also have proven genetic and linguistic roots in northern India, came to Europe together with the Roma and always kept certain shared habits (and suffered similar mistreatment) even while remaining apart from majority society. German cultural anthropologists have concluded that German Sinti already spoke a very different language from that of the Roma in the 14th century. [9]

Whereas Roma were and still are found all across Europe – as well as places as far as Australia, North and South America and South Africa – the Sinti historically had a smaller dispersal area. Sinti lived in or near German-speaking Europe. One should remember, however, that German-speaking Europe in the 1800s was more than only Germany, Austria and Switzerland. There were large German-speaking towns and communities in the Sudetenland (in today's Czech Republic), Hungary, Croatia, Russia, Ukraine and elsewhere. Some Sinti lived in France, Holland and northern Italy. Still, their geographic spread was never far from German communities. In the Romani language, one says that one speaks Romanes (the adverbial form of Romani). The Sinti also say that they speak Romanes, yet they do not speak the same language as Roma. The Sinti language is a creole, blending

Romani and German words and features (though, as mentioned, Sinti and Romani may have been very different long before the Sinti's language took on its German influences). Whereas Nazis and their partners targeted all Gypsies for genocide and while many Roma perished, the decimation of Sinti life and culture came especially close to its final aim. Today, people with Sinti identity outside of Germany and Austria are very rare. Slovenia's surviving community, though better researched and known than many, counts only 150 people. Once vibrant Sinti communities in many countries are not only gone but largely forgotten. In Germany, a small but proud Sinti community, including the Trollmann family, work hard to assure that the Sinti losses of the Holocaust do not disappear from historical memory.

Germany was not the worst place in Europe to be a Gypsy at the start of the twentieth century but Sinti and Roma did not enjoy full equality there. While they amounted to no more than 0.03% of the German population according to government data in 1910[10] and though many of them lived very normal lives, the majority view was that Gypsies were a problem. Germans believed Sinti and Roma to be criminals who refused to live like decent people. There were laws aimed specifically at Gypsies. From the 1880s until the Nazi ascent to power, government policies explicitly and differently addressed Gypsies, who were to be treated by law enforcement with discrimination.

In 1886, for example, the chancellor wrote to ministries to encourage them to enforce laws aimed specifically at Gypsies. In 1890, the Schwabian parliament had held a conference on "the Gypsy Vermin". The practice of ringing church bells to warn white Germans when Gypsies came to town was enforced by law. In the Weimar Republic, Roma were forbidden from entering public swimming pools, parks, and other recreational areas. Gypsies were usually depicted in media as criminals. A directive in 1906 in Prussia ordered that Gypsies should, when charged with any offense, be "punished without leniency". Discriminatory sentencing was the stated intent.

Germany and the region into which Johann Trollmann was born did not believe in racial equality or see Gypsies, who had lived there for countless generations, as Germans or as equals. It did not see them as equally German before the Nazis took power and, of course, did not consider them human during the Third Reich. When the authorities began to round up the Sinti and Roma for the Final Solution, historian Guenter Lewy says, "Very few Gypsies found refuge with non-Gypsy families...On the other hand, we...know of cases in which Gypsies were denounced to the police [for their deportation to the camps]."

Exceptions were not to be made. In February 1944 a Gypsy woman, Helene K. was taken by the authorities in Cologne, Germany for removal to Auschwitz. By June, the location of her two daughters, twelve and thirteen years old, was learned. They were in foster care with an Aryan family on a farm. Their legal guardian appealed to the court to keep them. Was there any appeal against their deportation to the camp, the foster family asked? The children had lived with their foster family for four years. They had displayed no criminal tendencies. The older child was a valuable worker on the farm. The reply was terse. These were mixed race Gypsy children and would be sent to Auschwitz. Final.

Sinti today carry the scars of the twentieth century. If their culture is less known and their voice unheard in European public debate, it is partly because the Sinti community is protective of its boundaries. As Romani Rose, the president of the German Sinti community's main organization, the Central Council of German Sinti and Roma, told Slovenian Sinto writer Rinaldo diRicchardi-Reichard, "The German Sinti concluded that teaching our culture be done only within Sinti families [and not publicly]...all of the German Associations of Sinti...have never spoken about their rules...such decisions have been made following the Second World War, after the Nazi regime."[11] In short, Sinti learned the hard way that trusting outsiders is dangerous. In the early twentieth century, some Sinti families welcomed anthropologists into their homes and hearts. They believed these researchers, who spent years getting to know and befriending the Sinti, could be trusted. Those same researchers provided information and validation to the Nazis as the policy of genocide was established and put into practice. Sinti leaders preach safety and clear limits. This is not to say that Sinti culture or language is a perfectly guarded secret. Bischoff's first Sinti-German dictionary was written in 1927. Mikhail Kogalniceanu's dictionary was put out in 1837. For the reader who wishes more deeply study Sinti culture, there are resources. Still, Sinti trepidation vis-à-vis the outside is strong and has been, since the 1940s, slow to fade.

In 1971 in London, a small number of Roma from a wide range of countries held a Gypsy World Congress. This meeting was the first step to the forming of the World Romani Congress in 1977 and eventually the International Romani Union (IRU), which would be the most visible international organization of Roma until the 1990s. (It still exists today, though it is no longer prominent as it was once and now shares turf with several international non-profits.) Sinti were in discussion with the participants of the many meetings and organizations but were not convinced to join. In time, Romani Rose and the Central Council of German Roma and Sinti chose to sever all ties with the IRU, seeing it as run by Roma from Communist and Socialist countries and hence incapable of political independence. Sinti remained for years outside of pan-European Romani activism. Even at the moment this is written, the largest consortium of Romani and other "Gypsy" community organizations in Europe, the European Roma and Travellers Forum has over one hundred representatives of Romani communities from over forty countries but not a single Sinto.

Times change, however, and Romani Rose and his organization are now – despite the objection of many members of the Sinti community – starting work with Romani activists across Europe. Rose, in 2015, joined the board of directors of a planned European Romani Institute to support academic research and media about Romani and Sinti cultures, arts and issues.

Aside from cooperation with Roma, as will be discussed, the organized Sinti community has, if nothing else, fought well for compensation for and the memory of Holocaust victims.

A Fighter's Roots

Rukeli was born on the morning of December 27, 1907 to Wilhelm and Friederike Trollmann. He was born in the apartment of the local barkeep. Wilhelm, illiterate, signed the birth certificate with three x's.

One of eight children, he was raised in poverty in a rough neighborhood in the city of Hannover. He grew up on crooked streets, among old and often dilapidated, municipally owned row houses. Friederike, or *Daju* (Momma in Sinti) stayed home. Rukeli's father, Wilhelm was known to family and friends as Schniplo for his cutting and carving skills. A veteran of the Great War, he made money where he could. He spent some time as an umbrella maker and worked for a while for the "water protection police". When furniture broke, Schniplo put his skills to use and tried to make repairs. He was resourceful and nothing was thrown away.

Schniplo and Friederike had married in 1901 in Hambergen and moved around the Hannover area for a few years before settling down. The Trollmanns had been in northern Germany for centuries and many were settled in one place a long time. Among them were puppeteers and professional musicians, knife sharpeners and basket makers. None of these occupations are unusual for Sinti or for Roma.

Daju smoked when she could get the tobacco, though never in the street. Cigarettes had only become common since the end of the Great War and were not yet sold by the pack in Germany. A woman smoking in public was rare (and would become illegal when the Nazis came to power). Daju already got enough looks just as a Gypsy woman, with her golden earrings and long black hair. She avoided drawing more attention through improper behavior. The family was cautious not to speak Sinti in public. They made efforts not to stand out.

The neighborhood's streets were a workplace for prostitutes and men walked through looking for action. Sometimes the Trollmann daughters received unwelcome looks and remarks. Rukeli and the other children played often with the Weiss children, who were also dark-skinned Sinti and lived nearby. They went swimming together in the nearby river, which always worried Daju. There was no reason to fear. Rukeli was a strong swimmer, a good athlete from the start.

When Rukeli first attended school, he was smacked for not responding when called upon. He had not realized that he was registered in school as Johann. Nobody had ever called him by his German name before. The white children's hair was short. He had wild, long black curls and holes in his shoes. However Rukeli and his siblings fit or did not fit at school, he and his brothers learned to read – mainly by teaching one another – and the girls did not.

Rukeli was not raised to be a star who stood along under a spotlight, but a member of a large ensemble, always sharing in the fun and sharing resources with his seven siblings. The eldest boy was Carlo. Say it with a German accent and it comes out "kahlo", which means black. He was the darkest of the children and responsible for the others. In the spring and fall, when farmers needed extra help the whole family would go off in a wagon they shared with relatives and seek itinerant labor. The children went to school wherever they stopped and found jobs if they could. Rukeli, his brother Mauso – three years younger – and brother Benni, a full seven years younger than Rukeli were all skinny and so they were shown off. Sympathy sometimes led to free meals. When work was unavailable and there was no charity, Schniplo sometimes resorted to stealing a rabbit or chicken. Roma and Sinti who travelled would leave each other signs along the roadsides, twisting leaves and branches – the very word for sign is *patrin* or leaf in Romani - to warn that the locals were mean spirited or to indicate that people were welcoming. Even today, as far away as North America, there are Gypsies who show their children how to read a *patrin* and even today, Sinti and Romani people use mutually intelligible signs.

At seven years old, Rukeli and his family lived at Haus Tiefenhal Number 5, a place with outdoor toilets and no running water. Nine families shared three outhouses. This was not because of the family's poverty. Apartment buildings in German cities at the time typically required tenants to share such facilities. When a child wanted to use a toilet, she would take a piece of old newspaper from the stairwell along with a key that hung there and go outside. The toilets were boards with holes in the middle.

Fuel and heat came from wood and coal when there was enough. The coal was kept in a box in the kitchen. In the summer, the box and stovepipe were put outside to make room.

Rukeli shared a bed with Carlo and with some bedbugs and mice. The city had plans to tear the building down and create housing for better off families. The Trollmanns and the other tenants lived with the awareness that the time to look for a new residence was always around the corner.

For the moment, then, this was home. The women cleaned clothes in a pot of hot water in the kitchen. Thinking back to the house, family members recall never having a key and having no need for one. Someone was always home. The family leased a garden nearby to grow beans. Most days they ate stews of beans, potatoes and whatever fat could be had. Without the garden, there would not have been enough. With the food they grew, there was still not much. The food was all cooked in one big, cast iron pan. Rukeli was not yet strong enough to pick it up. They often ate red sauerkraut, colored by tomatoes or red paprika. The paprika was crucial. Sinti liked their food spicier than other Germans did.

The school Rukeli attended was an all-boys' institution where teachers used corporal punishment. Rukeli was fast and, when he saw the teacher's hand coming, ducked it. This angered the authority figure and made things worse. His teacher did not like having the rest of the class laugh as the little Gypsy boy evaded his punishment.

Rukeli, when not going to school, caught hedgehogs to sell as food. For Sinti and Roma, a roasted hedgehog is a delicacy. Fattest in autumn when they are gaining weight for winter hibernation, they can be removed from their quills by punching a hole in the hide with a thin reed or needle and then blowing threw a reed or some kind of straw, inflating the carcass to separate the skin and prickles and easily remove them from the meaty body. Sinti and Roma roast the animal over a fire or stew it in a sauce. The Manouche have a tradition of cooking it in a clay jar, ideally with thyme and garlic before removing the prickles and hide. It is not a German custom to eat hedgehog but these were tough times and people in Rukeli's neighborhood ate the meat they could afford.

At night the family crowded into their narrow apartment. Rukeli looked out the window at the corner gas lamp. The gas lanterns had holes in the bottom. Early mornings a man with a pole came and put out the flame.

Rukeli was eight years old when he visited a boxing hall for the first time. A friend brought him to look around the local school's sports hall, where the friend had been training for a few weeks. Boxing was illegal, partly because many saw it as a foreign import, something English. And England, so few years after the Great War, was no friend. The few who boxed in Germany were the well traveled; sailors, traders, soldiers who had picked it up as prisoners of war. For a boy like Rukeli, there was something glamorous in it.

It was illegal and associated with rough types but here it was, this enticing, forbidden fruit and a chance to prove who was toughest. Carlo thought it was a bad idea to let his little brother get knocked about but their father saw no harm in learning to defend oneself. [12]

He started going to the sports hall on Schaufelder Street, walking the few kilometers when he could and jumping on a streetcar if the weather was bad. The streetcars were their own novelty and also controversial. Electric streetcars had just begun to replace horse-drawn mass transit in Hannover. Not all agreed it was progress and not all felt safe with the new means of transport. When it moved slowly through town, people jumped off and on at any point, meaning that young people stowed away as often as they paid their fares. One could always jump off at the first sight of a ticket collector. Rukeli rode this way.

When he showed up at the Schaufelder Street sports center to begin training, the older students shirked him. He looked too small, too frail. They sent him away and a few days later he returned. He had no tennis shoes or exercise clothes but he was back. They relented and gave him the tour of the gym.

A description of the training hall would not surprise anyone who knows today's boxing clubs. It was all new to the wide-eyed Rukeli. There was the smell of sweat, a changing room and a shower. Rukeli, who washed in a basin at home, had never seen one before. The other boys showed him how it worked.

In the boxers' training area, Rukeli found open spaces, a climbing wall, hooks that hung from the ceiling. There was no boxing ring. It was not always assembled but was put together when needed.

Gloves were handed out to the students. There was no equipment that the children needed to buy. If there had been, it might have been the newcomer's first and last time. Mouth protectors were not a norm yet in the sport. Rubber mouth guards were only starting to sell.

The boxers gathered around. It was time to test the new blood. Rukeli was hit in the face until his nose burst, swelling and bleeding. This was the first step to acceptance. One had to bleed and then choose to stick around for more.

He would have to come and work out for months before he was given his moment to enter the ring. When the chance came, he was not paired off with an easy win. He was put up against a boy a year and a half older and much bigger. Rukeli recalled later that he thought he won but the referee counted more points for the older boy. Trollmann was afraid the loss would mean that he could not come to train anymore.[13] The other boys patted him on the back and told him everyone has to lose sometimes. And learn from it.

The friend who first brought him soon quit. Rukeli would not. He was hooked.

In 1916, before turning nine, he had three fights behind him and made it as far as the South District Championship as a bantamweight (53 kilos, or 116 pounds). His ribs showing through his t-shirt, he was an emaciated little thing in a game for hearty, properly nourished boys. He lost but learned from the experience. He went on, in the years ahead, to win the district title four times.

In 1919 the ban on boxing, already unenforced and the source of sports hall jokes, ended. In 1920 the German Reich Association for Amateur Boxing was established and in 1922 the *Hannover Heroes Boxing Club* was formed. Germany, seen as the aggressor in the Great War, was excluded from the 1920 and 1924 Olympics. Yet Germans needed distraction as much as ever and, in a country where so much was uncertain and where poverty and unemployment led to so many humiliations, many turned to a sport that offered the chance to show one's strength.

In 1922, Foreign Minister Walter Rathenau, the highest-ranking Jew in the German government was assassinated. It was two months after he had signed the Treaty of Rapallo, by which Germany and the Soviet Union put aside unresolved financial and territorial claims from the war. He was in his convertible, being driven from his home in Berlin-Grunewald to the Foreign Office when a Mercedes pulled up next to him. One of the men in the other car shot him with an MP 18 sub-machine gun, the kind that German soldiers had carried in the war. The Foreign Minister was killed instantly but the murderers took no chances, throwing a grenade into his car. The men in the car were arrested mere days later. One, Ernst Werner Techow claimed in court that Rathenau had admitted to be being one of the evil *Elders of the Protocols of Zion*, referring to the fictional but widely believed anti-Semitic book that was so popular in Germany (and was simultaneously being distributed in the U.S. by Henry Ford). Rathenau soon became an icon for those who worried about preservation of democracy in Germany. Whatever his eventual value in death as a symbol for anti-fascists, the assassination succeeded in adding chaos and fear to a fragile system, weakening the regime.

Life in Hannover and across Germany grew rapidly harder. In 1923 unemployment rose and businesses closed. The poor became poorer and inflation left people wondering what good their savings would do them. In November, Adolph Hitler led a *putsch*. Interrupting the head of the Bavarian state during a speech in a beer hall in Munich,

Hitler fired a pistol into the air and, with several armed soldiers backing him up, declared: "The national revolution has begun!" Several of his supporters, a bystander and four police officers died before order was restored and two days passed before Hitler was found and taken into custody.

Two hundred members of the Nazi party demonstrated in his favor on Georg Street in Hannover. Police did not interfere. When he was finally jailed, crowds cheered for Hitler.

In 1924, he and his colleagues were put on trial in Bavaria for treason. He used the media attention to announce clearly to national media that he aimed to overthrow the Weimar Republic. The location of his bold statement was well chosen, as local politicians in Bavaria had stood repeatedly against the government in Berlin. When he said that he and the people in charge had "the same goal…to get rid of the Reich government" he did not sound crazy. He sounded like a plain-spoken voice for change from dysfunctional politics. He was given five years in prison, the minimum sentence for his crime and was released in far less time, before Christmas of that same year. Hitler later said: "The failure of the putsch was perhaps the greatest good fortune of my life."[14]

In 1925 Rukeli won his first district title, as a middleweight.

Boxing Comes Out

What was this sport that had just come out of the shadows, and who were the boxers?

New to Germany, boxing had long been an established sport in Britain. By the seventeenth century in England, nobility patronized the fights. Matches were held in a square ring, marked by staked ropes and usually outdoors. The first recorded champion was James Figg, who also won contests with the sword and cudgel.[15] He beat all adversaries at an amphitheater in London, competing at the same time as the somewhat better remembered Benjamin Boswell, whose family claimed to be Romani royalty. Boswell was a known highwayman as well as a pugilist. One of the fight sport's first chroniclers, Captain John Godfrey wrote that Boswell had "a particular blow with his left hand at the jaw, which comes almost as hard as a little horse kicks". Romanies were prominent in early British boxing and Romani fighters were heroes among their people. "Gypsy Jack" Cooper, another early champion was so infamous that even today, Romani and caravan people in the UK will sometimes ask a vain man, "Who do you think you are, Gypsy Jack?"

The Marquess of Queensberry was the first to codify rules for boxing with gloves. Soon bare-fisted boxing was made illegal and driven underground. There, it would continue among Romani and nomadic communities as well as a few others, such as in certain mining towns, where athletes and audiences kept tournaments under the radar but very much alive.

In the U.S. in the 1800s, boxing drew growing numbers of participants and fans. Popular as a spectator event at travelling circuses and fairs, fight sports drew many Roma and Sinti, as these communities were heavily involved in the circus business and in the horse dealing that was an important part of many fairs. The English heavyweight champion in 1870, a Romani man named Jem Mace travelled to Louisiana to beat the American, Tom Allen. If not sanctioned by the law, such events drew crowds and bettors.

There were few international or trans-Atlantic sports celebrities outside of boxing. Though not legal everywhere it drew audiences, the sport was unusual for its crowning of world champions whose pictures appeared in newspapers across borders.[16] The first World Heavyweight Boxing Championship title was awarded in the 1880s to John "The Boston Strong Boy" Sullivan.

In 1889 the last bareknuckle heavyweight title match was held in an outdoor ring in Mississippi. Sullivan beat Jake Kilrain at the end of seventy-five rounds. Read that again; seventy-five rounds. Records are not available to tell us how many bones in their hands were broken when the fight concluded. With such practices stopped, it did not take long for professional boxing, with gloves and the Marquess of Queensberry's rules, to become legal in New York in 1896, the shaky start of acceptance in the New World. The law was repealed in 1900, stopping the business until it was returned to legality in 1911. In 1917, a year before Rukeli first stepped into a boxing gym, New York again drove the sport underground and in 1920 again allowed it with the passing of the Walker Law.

Through the 1920s, minorities dominated American boxing (and still do). Unlike in so many sports in the U.S., Blacks were generally allowed to participate, though there were many whites, including champion John Sullivan, who refused to enter the ring with them and many Black fighters competed in a separate circuit, with its own Colored Champions. Sullivan also refused to compete against Jews or other "non-white" athletes.

Boxing's first Black heavyweight champion was Jack Johnson, who reigned with a rare style built around counterpunches from 1908 to 1915. Born in Galveston, Texas, the son of a freed slave, Johnson started his fighting career in "Battle Royals". African American men were blindfolded and then fought in a rules-free group encounter to the cheers of white spectators. No one-on-one competition, it was a free-for-all until only one was standing.

He would eventually become World Colored Heavyweight Champion, defending the title seventeen times before successfully convincing a white champion to let him compete for the mainstream title.

Tommy Burns agreed to fight Johnson for the World Heavyweight Title in 1908 in Sydney, Australia. Race was not the only factor Burns ignored. Johnson outweighed him by roughly 30 pounds and was six inches taller. Today there would be several weight divisions between them. Burns lasted fourteen rounds before police pulled the boxers apart and Johnson won the title.

When not preparing for a fight, he toured as a celebrity act in vaudeville shows, flaunting his jewelry and wealth before shadow boxing for audiences. He infuriated much of the public, especially in the states where he spent the most time, by socializing with and marrying white women, even at a time when other African American men were lynched for similar transgressions.

Johnson died at the age of sixty-six. Friends recount that at a restaurant in Raleigh, North Carolina he had been told that he and his party were only welcome to sit in the back, where Colored diners were permitted. He walked out to his car, a Lincoln Zephyr, sped away and died after a high-speed crash friends believed was caused by his rage at the insult.[17]

However notable Johnson's success in the ring, Jews were the minority whom the fighting sport drew in greatest numbers in its early years of legality. Many competed internationally. From 1910-1940, there were twenty-six Jewish world champions. These titles were competitive. There were only eight weight classes, far fewer than the many classes today and there was none of today's complex web of sanctioning bodies. A title-holder truly was the undisputed best in his class. By 1928, the majority of pro fighters in America were Jewish, followed by Irish-Americans. In the 1920s and 1930s, about a third of the fighters in the U.S. were Jewish. The 5'5" Jewish Benjamin Leiner, who fought as Benny Leonard, "the Ghetto Wizard" with a Jewish star on his trunks, reigned as the world lightweight champion from 1917 to 1925. Benny Leonard was fighting Lew Tendler Jr. when overhead lights were first used for a night fight, at Yankee Stadium in the summer of 1923.

One might wonder whether the Jewish fighters had something to prove. Jimmy Johnston, a promoter of the period once said: "You take a Jewish boy and sooner or later his race is decried. He tries much harder to fight back for himself...the knowledge that more than one Jew is on trial when he fights gives him incentive." Neither European nor American society was free of hostility. While Henry Ford disseminated the *Protocols of the Elders of Zion*, Harvard University and other top universities in the U.S. set limits on the number of Jews they would admit. Discrimination in employment and housing were taken as natural. Jewish American journalist Ben Hecht commented on life in Germany from 1918-1920 that "there was less anti-Semitism to be heard, seen...than at any time in the U.S.A."[18]

Then again, most of the boxers may have been fighting less to prove a point than to make a living. These were not young men who chose between boxing and college, or boxing and much else at all. New York's and America's Jewish population was made primarily of manual laborers and first and second generation Americans who lived below the middle class. These were not people who had it easy. In 1911, seventy-two percent of New York's prostitutes were Jewish. They were also probably not focusing on making any point.

The boxers did not live in a society free of bigotry, yet anti-Semitism was not a consistent issue in the business, as it was not only the men stepping into the ring who were Jewish. It was everyone in their world. Jews were present as trainers, managers, promoters. The Everlast Company, the pre-eminent provider of boxing equipment was founded by Russian Jewish immigrants. "The predominance of fans were the Jews" as well according to Vic Zimet, who was a manager and trainer during the period.[19] And boxing had a history, even before it had been legalized in Germany or in the U.S., as a sport where what mattered was what the fighter could do. This was not only true for Romani people in Britain. Daniel Mendoza, also a Jew, had been England's champion from 1791 to 1795. That too had been a time and place in which Jews were not welcome at the top of all professions.

The center of the pro boxing scene was New York, which was also the center of America's Jewish community. Charley Phil Rosenberg fought in Ohio a month after winning the world bantamweight title at Madison Square Garden. Someone siting ringside kept shouting to his opponent to "kill the Jew bastard" and Rosenberg could not take anymore. After he got up from his corner stool, leaned over the ropes and spat a mouth full of water, saliva and blood into the man's eyes, he learned who it was - the mayor of Toledo. Minority boxers in America were not isolated from the attitudes of the time. They simply found a profession in which it did not decide their fates.

The culture in which boxing existed was not only different from today's in regard to attitudes about ethnicity. Attitudes about boys hitting and getting hit were also different. Charles Gellman, a middleweight at the time recalls, "I came home with a couple [of bruises], but it was normal. Everybody was in a street fight in those days. There was a guy in the firehouse nearby, he would give you a pair of gloves and he'd watch."

While it may be strange today to picture a firefighter, a public servant encouraging children to settle arguments by physical force while he watched the show, it was the norm. Charlie Nelson grew up in an orphanage in New York's Hell's Kitchen. The priests who took care of him would order boys who argued to resolve their differences with boxing gloves. There was apparently nothing un-Christian about letting might determine right.

In Germany, boxing was quickly rising in popularity. Pugilism clubs affiliated with political parties sprung up. There was for a time no sport that could claim to be the national pastime – soccer was also a recent import from the English-speaking world – and boxing had as much chance as any athletic activity to become the national passion. Fencing had long been important among the university-educated and the upper crust but it was not for everyone. It was elite in terms of its image and the cost of learning. Boxing was a common man's game.

While Gypsies were not much present in New York's professional boxing world, they took to it wherever they were and to whatever form of pugilism they encountered. In 1920 a ten-year-old Manouche who would one day become Europe's most famous Gypsy and one of the world's most famous jazzmen, Django Reinhardt punched it out with other boys for spectators' tips in a boxing ring at a café on the avenue d'Italie in Paris.[20]

Texas-based Sinto-Romani American Aaron Williams (no relation to the famous athlete) tells of his grandfather, Joe Schwartz boxing for pay in the American West in 1898. His other grandfather, Otto Wells ran a traveling boxing ring that served as an attraction within circuses and fairs. One of Williams' uncles performed in exhibition matches; given local interests at the time, he was not billed as a Gypsy but as a Native American. Among the Sinti who came to the U.S. in the 1800s, many took work in circuses or travelling shows, and these often included some kind of pugilism or wrestling. There were many fighting styles and sets of rules, usually bare knuckles. According to Williams, Joe Schwartz fought outdoors or on dirt floors. Scratch marks on the ground indicated the ring and fighters lost if they retreated or were beaten past their scratch lines.

The Sinti in Williams' family tree mingled so much with Romnitchels, or English Romani immigrants in America that they soon stopped referring to themselves as Sinti. They came to be known as "Dutch Romnitchels" or "Black Dutch". "Lots of the Romnitchels still do it," he says of closed-door boxing tournaments. The unsanctioned, illegal competitions are today held all across the West and Midwest and bring together Gypsy men who rarely interact otherwise. For example, he says, "It's the only place some of them meet up with the Irish Gypsies." Any of the Romanitchels and Sinti in places like Oklahoma, Texas and the West who fought for a crowd in the 1920s or 1930s would have been doing it in clandestine events. Legalized boxing came later to that part of country.

The unsanctioned but widely attended bareknuckle competitions continued in the UK and Ireland as well, especially among Gypsies. Even today, such contests are often discretely organized at fairs where caravan people gather, like Appleby in northwestern England, Musselburgh in Scotland or Ballinasloe in Ireland and, on a smaller scale, at caravan sites.[21] Sometimes there are rules similar to those of gloved boxing. Sometimes there are few rules at all.

And Romani and other Gypsy people continue to participate in mainstream boxing. 2015 World Heavyweight Boxing Champion Tyson Fury says of his Gypsy culture: "Before anything else, you learn how to fight. Whereas in other cultures little kids will kick a ball about, we're punching hands."[22]

Lean and Hard Years

Europe was recovering slowly from the Great War and struggling to rebuild economically. Django Reinhardt's mother, abandoned by her husband Jean-Eugene Weiss (a very rare disgrace in the Manouche community), fed her boy by collecting used artillery shell casings on the battlefield of the Marne in France. She taught Django to spot them in the old trenches, to wash them and repurpose the brass into bracelets with engravings.

Failing to make due with such projects, the Reinhardts moved from mainland France to colonial Algeria. In the casbah of Algiers, they found a neighborhood under the shadow of the Grand Mosque where recently arrived Manouche from Europe mingled with "Afrikaya" Gypsies, as the Manouche who had abandoned France for the periphery generations earlier were called, as well as with Muslim nomads from other parts of North Africa. They wrestled with their options and hunted for ways to survive. When Django was ten they moved again, back to Paris. At the age of twelve, he acquired a banjo and began teaching himself to play it. A few months later, he was working until dawn as a performer in nightclubs and dance halls, keeping company with prostitutes and pimps until closing time, when his mother collected him and brought him back to their caravan site to sleep.

As people sought out creative ways to earn their bread in the countries that had won the last war, things were even harder on the losing side. Germany's economy worsened. The Trollmanns survived. Rukeli's older brothers worked. His father and sisters traveled and sought day labor on farms. At times they begged. In 1923, national consumption of wheat had fallen by half. In October, women stormed the Hannover city hall in protest. People who could not afford meat bought bones to give some meat flavor to their stews of locally found vegetables like cabbage. Before long, bread became unaffordable.

While many went to municipal kitchens for free meals, Rukeli got a sandwich after workouts and a hot meal after a fight at the sports hall. The association fed its protégés. Fighting was already how Johann Trollmann earned his bread.

Children Rukeli's age were disappearing from the Old Town. In February of 1924 the first bones were removed from the Leine river. In May, children discovered a skull in a pond. Soon police would find the bones of twenty-two victims, mostly young boys. In June, Friedrich Haarman was arrested. Haarman had been living in the Engel family inn and had been helping to find "horse meat" for its kitchen, as well as used clothes for the Engels. This went on until the mother of one of the missing boys recognized her child's coat on Mrs. Engel's son. Hannover was traumatized. People were desperate for change. Rukeli was not lucky to eat; he earned his food through hard training. He was, however, lucky not to be eaten.

At least Rukeli and the other boys and men who boxed had somewhere to go and to lose themselves in their efforts. In 1926 there were forty-five boxing clubs in northwest Germany, with more than two thousand members. A year later, the number grew to sixty-six associations with 3,552 members. Mass media took interest. Professional boxers could become stars, none bigger than Max Schmeling.

Boxers were tough and brave. Their success, unlike so much in the Weimar Republic, could not come from connections or family inheritance. A boxer won on his own two feet and not by connections. After the war, soldiers were defeated and their manhood diminished. Boys needed heroes and boxing offered them. The rising political figure, Hitler took notice and became an enthusiastic fan. As he put it, "If our upper class had learned boxing, a German revolution of pimps, deserters and other such rubbish wouldn't be possible."

In 1920 the German Worker Party was renamed the National Socialist German Workers' Party, or NSDAP. The Nazis, in their renaming and restructuring, created a Gymnastics and Sports Section. Hitler and the party espoused the importance not only of athletic competition but also of building all young German men's aggression and a warrior spirit. Boxing, more than any other sport, appealed to

Hitler and the Nazis and was recommended to young recruits. In the years when the party was forbidden from direct involvement in certain political activities, Hitler oversaw the creation of a *Sportabteilung* (SA) or Sports Battalion that encouraged young supporters to learn boxing and other sports. The S.A. was in charge of the security of senior party members at rallies and events, and starting fights at opposing parties' gatherings. Hitler enjoyed keeping his SA around and encouraged the organization to recruit boxers and to train in the sport. In Hannover, there were several SA members with boxing backgrounds. After the party was renamed and after an infamous gang fight in Munich, it seemed Hitler might reign in the young thugs. Instead, he embraced their more overt and threatening public image. He rebranded the SA as the *Sturmabteilung* (Storm Battalion), going well beyond the sports orientation and hinting that destruction and chaos were their purpose.

Of course the challenges and pride of boxing did not only appeal to the growing fascist community. It was a sport that touched on the needs of people facing hardship. There is something meditative and calming about a boxer's training. One cannot work that hard physically and one cannot spar, concentrate on an attacker, while thinking of other things. A fighter's mind has its focus and its purpose. "Boxing" writes Norman Mailer, "is the exclusion of outside influence." How precious that must have made the boxing hall in 1920s Germany, where outside influences and the confusion of defeat and loss were so overwhelming. Roger Repplinger puts it: "What had seemed absolute in the Kaiser's time was not. The Kaiser is gone. He is in exile…this hurts some people. God went with the Kaiser into exile…in the Weimar Republic, Protestantism lost its leading role….women with short hair, colorful dancers without much [clothing] on…homosexuality, abstract painting, Jazz, cocaine…boxing matches are a vent for this overheated society…On the other hand, boxing also adds heat…much clearer than the rest of life." [23]

It was not the only or the craziest fad gaining momentum. Germans were seeking something to fill a gap. Chicago journalist Edward Mowrer and his wife Lilian, living in Berlin in the 1920s reflected on a country going through profound doubt and confusion. "Where but in Germany could one find 150,000 organized nudists?"[24] he asked. Lilian worried about the "loose emotional fervor" of the nudist movement, noting its ardent yearning for something different. Most of the young people" she wrote, were "Communist...those feelings...could be just as easily canalized and turned in any other direction by an unscrupulous leader". She asked her husband "Do you think Germans are madder than any other people? They seem so...hysterical."

Edgar answered that "there is almost nothing they can't persuade themselves to believe".

> *"Hitler took very little interest in educational questions...The only time he did produce a real suggestion...was in 1935, I believe, when he told me that I should see to it that boxing become more widespread among youth."*
>
> **-Baldur von Schirach, former head of the Hitler Youth, speaking at the Nuremburg trials**

Rukeli Finds His Style

Hannover began to produce its share of good boxers. The city's Heinrich Brofazi would take a bronze medal at the European Championships in 1927. He had shared the ring with Rukeli, though by the European Championships they no longer competed in the same weight class. Rukeli had grown. Others from the Heroes Club, like Erich Wilke, did well in international competitions and would become national champions. It was normal for young boys to compete, even against older athletes. The issue was one's ability and not one's age, with no rule to define a boxer's entry into adulthood.

In 1925 Karl Leyendecker became the club's trainer. He was a charismatic figure for young boys in search of inspiration. He had been a pilot in the last war and been injured. The job was part of an effort to assure that wounded combat veterans had employment. Under him, training was a fast and intense two-hour session. Twenty to thirty trainees lined up by height and counted off. He spaced them out to give each of them room to work. They did calisthenics as Leyendecker shouted. They did shadow boxing to practice combinations. He watched them slip imaginary punches. "Roll the torso", he barked. "Again." He ordered them to practice hooks, uppercuts. He had them jump rope. They rotated, taking turns on a solitary heavy bag. To find a good trainer took some real luck, as there were plenty of men with no serious training in the sport who gave lessons. Rukeli and the boys at Heroes were lucky. Leyendecker, in fact, also was merely self-taught but he was, as it turned out, a good autodidact. He could do more than keep his fighters working and sweating as some self-proclaimed boxing experts did. He could see talent. He noticed Johann Trollmann right away and kept a careful eye on him during sparring. When Rukeli had a fight, the trainer liked to go along to stay in his corner, and to carry his spit bucket. He chastised Rukeli at times, especially for not keeping his fists up where they could best protect his face yet there was no missing the student's discipline, his willingness to do as instructed or his raw talent.

Rukeli himself was aware that he had an aptitude. He knew that he was better than boys who had trained longer. The others respected him. He was the only Sinto but many of them lived in similar conditions of poverty. It was not a discriminatory environment, at least not according to the benchmarks of the time.

Rukeli learned to present openings as bait. He learned to watch his opponent's eyes and to see what was coming. He developed his own style and Leyendecker did not try to force conformity. Perhaps as a self-taught aficionado, he never considered that there was an orthodox style, one right way that everyone should practice. In any case, Rukeli was allowed to find his own best form. As Repplinger writes, he boxed "slyly like a fox…devious…boxing is both about hitting and avoiding…he notices they are equally important."

His style was about centered, calm performance. Angry fighters made mistakes.

He was not in it to show that he could take a beating. He was there to get food, and maybe in time to really earn a living from it. As he began to earn, he became important to the club. The Heroes would hold twenty events in a year and arrange three or more foreign trips for matches. Rukeli was part of a group of fighters hungry for opportunities to enter the ring.

In 1925 Hitler published his manifesto, *Mein Kampf*. In it, he advocates boxing. "Boxing and Jiu-Jitsu have always appeared more important to me…give the German nation six million sporty, impeccable, trained bodies, all glowing from fanatical love of Fatherland and trained to the highest fighting spirit, and a national state will come from them… the creation of an army."

By this same year, the eighteen-year-old Rukeli was the amateur district champion for his weight class and enjoyed some local fame. He worked at times but mostly trained and sometimes benefactors helped him, giving him money to keep him honing himself in the sports hall.

He collected friends and fans but also some complaints. Those who lost were not happy about it. Speaking much later, some fans have reminisced and compared his footwork to Mohammed Ali's. His way of moving within the ring looked nothing like the norm of the time. People said he was tricky. They said he feinted too much. There was no name for his style and some people prefer what can be labeled. Still, he was working on techniques and strategies that worked for him, and he saw a career for himself in that much-discussed footwork.

Rukeli learned to throw punches – and to land them – while retreating. He worked on a distracting and effective left jab. He avoided fighting from the inside, getting close. He was quick on his feet and kept safe distances. Observers said he was a dancer. Those who wanted to see two fighters stand and exchange blows, those who knew nothing of technique and just wanted to see bruisers draw blood were not his fans. Some did appreciate his unusual moves. In 1928 the Berlin *Box-Sport* newspaper, the most important of the German boxing press mentioned him for the first time. Trollmann, it said, could be likeable and said that he "showed himself in every way a fair sportsman."

Still, in a country where boxing was new one can suppose that audiences were more likely to appreciate a barroom brawl than a subtle, footwork-based style. It is not only that the sport was new. There was precedent, the German tradition of the dueling scar. Among men of the upper classes, there was no higher sign of an elite upbringing than the scar from Heidelberg-style dueling. Only men of the right families were admitted to these clubs. Fencing clubs in general did not admit Jews. Gypsies were so rare at universities that rules about their admission to fencing clubs were not needed. The Heidelberg style was even more elite than fencing overall. Unlike in normal fencing, this game required the swordsmen to wear protective masks that left the cheeks exposed. Footwork was not allowed. A step back meant surrender and shame. One fenced until the face was bloody and scarred. Winning the match was not the most important thing about a Heidelberg fencing bout. The proof of having been through the ritual was the prize. Where, to people who had grown up with this ideal, was the honor of a boxer who liked to win and did not take pride in showing how much abuse he could take along the way?

Boxing, of course, was not for the country's upper classes. It was for a much larger audience and Rukeli's fans kept coming to see him.

His younger brother Stabeli was playing violin and aimed to make a living as a musician. The family's small apartment poured the sounds of his practicing into the halls and out onto the street day and night. Carlo, Lolo and Mauso did manual labor when they could find it. Rukeli's little brother Benni, still in school, was starting to come to the sports hall, as were many other Sinti boys with dreams of following in Rukeli's footsteps. He had made a wave.

In 1926, while Django Reinhardt first heard jazz music played on a mixture of drum, trumpets, saxophones and clarinets by African American performers at a restaurant on the place Pigalle in Paris, and while Rukeli helped his brother to lace on his boxing gloves and to see if he had his big brother's gift, the "Law for the Fight Against Gypsies, Vagrants and the Work-shy" was enacted in Bavaria. It stipulated that Gypsies could not travel to the region. Making a living in any way that required going long distances to the client was "asocial" behavior; more accurately, traveling to make a living was asocial, but only when the traveler was of the wrong ethnicity. Still, traveling for work and for sport to most parts of Germany would not be a problem. Never mind Bavaria. Life went on.

In 1928 Rukeli fought as a middleweight against Franz Lenkheit from Hamburg. Box-Sport called the fight "a delicacy", a special treat for the true enthusiast. His fight, it said, "against the experienced Lenkheit...[was] well thought out. He used his bodily strength in every way, put everything into his punch and could on several occasions force Lenkheit onto the defense...At times Lenkheit, the northwestern German champion had the advantage. The last round deciding the encounter...for Trollmann... [with] an upward hook that Trollmann sent through Lenkheit's defenses."

Though amateur, Trollmann continued to earn from his wins. Business owners gave him money. He learned to enjoy pocket cash. He had to help his family and was quick to help others. He came to be remembered by Sinti for his generosity to all children who needed something to eat. After all the attention to others, Rukeli still had enough that he was able to spend something on entertainment. He went to motorcycle races when he could afford it. Outdoor races went from 6 a.m. to 1.30 p.m. He brought his brothers and sometimes his father. Rukeli spoke often of one day buying a motorcycle, though they were not within the boxer's reach.

Motor races were not his only hobby. A single young man, he liked to go roller skating places and to the dance halls. He liked the Neue Haus on King Street and he loved the Fledermaus, where waiters wore red tailcoats. His favorite, closer to home in the Old Town, was the Markthalle. It was a steel and iron building with electric lights, an elevator and even flushing toilets. Sometimes a fan bought him a beer, poured into a tall *stein* and there was always the pleasure of girl watching.

This was the year when Django Reinhardt, in France, made his first studio recordings, at the age of 18. At a studio in Paris' Pigalle neighborhood, he played banjo to accompany a musician named Vaissade's accordion and another man playing the *jazzflute*, a kind of slide whistle for a number of waltzes and light opera airs.

In Berlin, S. Miles Boulton, the Baltimore Sun correspondent reported that the songs about spilling Jewish blood were often sung by uniformed marchers with swastikas.

As Django recorded and the Nazis sang, Rukeli, aged nineteen, fought his one hundredth match. It was summer and he was booked to fight at the Police Sports Association's open-air event. According to Box-Sport, his fight was the main event. Fighting middleweight, he won on points. Box-Sport wrote that "he didn't completely exploit his chances... Still, T. is clever enough to duck precarious situations. The point victory was given to Trollmann. On the occasion of his one hundredth fight, this victory was suitably honored by the association."

Later in the year, Rukeli became the northwestern regional middleweight champion and qualified for the national championships, to be held in Leipzig.

There in Leipzig, he lost to Bernhard Skibinski. The loss meant that Rukeli would not be nominated to the 1928 Olympic team, a goal that had been on his mind for some time. As the renowned Austrian playwright Felix Mitterer puts it ominously in *Der Boxer*, "*Rukeli wird noch viele schone Kampfe bestreiten*":[25] Rukeli had yet many great fights ahead of him.

Not all who were opposed to him as a candidate for the Olympic team were interested in the loss in Leipzig. There were others who raised questions about his character, claiming that he had a criminal record. A police certificate of good conduct was obtained to clear his name. Even with proof that the rumors of a criminal connection were nonsense, not everyone saw him as an appropriate representative of Germany. None mentioned race openly as a factor. They preferred, for the moment, to question his "character".

Functionaries in amateur boxing's leadership argued at length about the choice of Olympic competitors. A few even fought in favor of Trollmann. An article appeared in the sports section of the *Hannover Allgemein* newspaper on the inconsistencies in the nominations for the Olympics.

Munich's Albert Leidmann went to the Olympics in the middleweight class and did not perform well, losing to the Belgian Léonard Steyaert.

Rukeli beat Leidmann in Hannover that same year. In October, Rukeli made his last amateur appearance for Heroes and again won. He then joined the Worker Sport Club, or *Arbeiterboxverein*. The term *worker* in this context does not mean in this context that the club was exclusively for professional athletes. Rather, it was a club intended to bring together members of the working class. In the worker sports clubs, all competitors received a certificate. There were no medals or badges. Even more of a direct challenge to societal norms, there would be no hymns sung. It was not a nationalist environment. Rukeli's decision was not quite a political one, nor void of political significance. Having seen a few things, he was developing a political disposition, though he did not join any party and never would.

He had seen the usual ways of sports organizing. Associations were run by middle class, middle-aged men, who recruited young, working class kids and managed them. The worker sport movement, founded in the 1890s, was intended as an alternative. In time, it would attract 1.3 million members and operate sixty newspapers. In 1929 in Hannover, over 133,000 "worker athletes" participated in 77 clubs.

In 1929 the governmental Centre for the Fight Against Gypsies in was opened. This body enforced restrictions on travel for undocumented Roma and Sinti and allowed arbitrary arrest and detention of Gypsies as a "means of crime prevention". The first site in Germany to be called a concentration camp was also opened in 1929, years before the Nazis' arrival in power. In Frankfurt, city officials had been discussing what to do with a settlement of Gypsy caravan residents in the Gallus quarter. Their current encampment was called dirty by white neighbors. It lacked sewage system or running water and there had been complaints that the children went to school unacceptably dirty. There was a debate about putting the children into a segregated class, turned down only because it would have cost additional money.

In September 1929, the city set up what it called a "concentration camp for Gypsies" outside the city, near the border with the state of Hesse. The *konzentrationslager* was fenced in but was not a prison. The residents came and went as they wished. The nearby town of Bad Vilbel protested. These were not the sorts of people they wanted for neighbors. In a Frankfurt city council meeting, delegates discussed how to handle the situation. One Communist member of the council got up to say that the Gypsies ought to be treated better. He said that in the Soviet Union former nomads were becoming well-adjusted citizens under a system of government that treated people of all races as equals. The assembly laughed.[26]

An investigation in 1930 found that no well for drinking water had yet been dug at the site. In fact, it was no better than the accommodations out of which the Sinti residents had been pushed. There was no school at all for the children. The idea that they had been moved for their own good was a farce. They had simply been swept out of Frankfurt and under the rug. The problem went away when the residents did; the Gypsies finally simply moved away from the area.

Municipal campsites for caravan-dwelling Sinti and Roma were established in other cities across Germany, such as Kiel and Freiburg. In some cases, the residents were obliged to relocate to them. Some of the campsites were fenced in and in other cases they were not. For the moment, there was a move to isolate Sinti and Roma who lived in caravans but nothing more. In later years, the nature of these same sites would change and they would become more like our modern understanding of the term *concentration camp*.[27]

> *"Life is like boxing in many unsettling respects. But boxing is only like boxing."*
>
> -Joyce Carol Oates

At the Worker Sport Club's Box Club Sparta Linden, Rukeli raised some eyebrows. He built a ring in Linden's Pfarrlandplatz and worked out in public as well as allowing competitions in the ring. This was not where or how other club members trained and the showy move struck some fellow club members as vain. On the other hand, when he boxed in public he drew an audience of 1,500 or more.

Professional martial arts fighter Forrest Griffin writes of his experience with audiences: "There are two ways to win the crowd. The first way is to be one of the best fighters on the planet. I'm not talking about a good fighter…you have to look so good when you're fighting that people think you're not even trying. You have to look like…if you were to pull it out, you'd start killing people left and right…[or, second] be more like me…a guy who seems to work for everything. Show expression and how hard you're working in every movement." Rukeli, while not Germany's or the world's greatest fighter, was introducing the boxing fans of Germany to the former, the pugilist who seems to be effortless. The young Gypsy made beating the White Man look easy. People were mesmerized and showed up even just to see him practice.

He was ready to decide to make boxing his life. In June 1929, he left the association and the club to become a professional fighter. Ernst Zirzow, a manager and small ring promoter in Berlin had offered him a contract and it was time to make the leap. The leading professional fighter in his weight class, Erich Seelig had already taken him on as a trainee. With Seelig, a Jew who became a champion in multiple weight classes, as a new coach and with the Berliner Zirzow negotiating the pay, it seemed there were big things ahead. The Worker Sport Clubs' days were in any case numbered, though few knew it at the time.

He picked a good time to demand to be paid for his boxing. There were not many other ways to earn. More businesses closed than opened. By September 1931, the Hannover Wagon Company (HAWA), one of the most important employers in Hannover would shut its doors indefinitely while seeing legal resolution of issues with its creditors. Other large employers would have layoffs and closures.

Between October and December 1929, he had his first three professional matches. He fought twice in the Spichernsälen in Berlin and once in Hannover's town hall. He won them all. He beat welterweight Willy Bolze on points, with the fight stopped at four rounds. He knocked out welterweight Alex Tomkowiak in the first round. These were exactly the sorts of first fights an early pro should have if his manager is thinking of his career. He fought good boxers but people for whom he was clearly ready, building confidence and reputation. Forrest Griffin puts it, "I recommend not biting off more than you can chew right off the bat. If a promoter is trying to match you up with someone who has twenty fights under his belt, unless he's lost nineteen of them, you'll probably want to find someone more on your level."[28]

Rukeli, while building experience so that he could handle that opponent with twenty wins, also built up earnings for himself and for Zirzow. He began to fight anyone his manager wanted, regardless of weight and he filled in for other fighters when they were sick. In short, he quickly transitioned to taking any payday, versus any opponent.

In 1930 he took thirteen fights, an unusual pace that left the fighter with no time for recovery from the injuries that can be expected in every bout, not to mention in training. In January he was knocked out by the national middleweight champion, Erich Tobeck and yet he waited no time before setting up his next fight. In more recent years, U.S. states like New York have imposed an automatic 90-day suspension for recovery on any fighter who is knocked out. These were not the norms in Rukeli's boxing world. Injuries were like the exhaustion of hard workouts. They were part of the landscape; obstacles to get around in order to win.

He continued to hone his nimble style. Even if Zirzow hounded him to go on the offensive, Rukeli listened to his own judgment on when to duck and when to engage. And he learned to fight from the inside, even if it was never his preference. He avoided corners, moved away from the ropes and danced away.

For the excitedly shouting crowds who came to watch, he was unusual and it was not only his moves that drew the eye. There were not many dark faces like his under German spotlights. He was exotic. Always jumping over the ropes to enter the ring, he threw kisses to women in the stands. The press remarked that women had never shown up to watch boxing before Rukeli came along.

If there was something exciting about his alien looks, it surely was also threatening in increasingly xenophobic Germany. Joyce Carol Oates sees boxing as a mirror: "The boxer meets an opponent who is a dream-distortion of himself...his weaknesses...all can be interpreted as strengths belonging to the Other...my strengths are not fully my own, but my opponent's weaknesses; my failure is not fully my own, but my opponent's triumph. He is my shadow-self..."[29] How unsettling it must have been in a defeated, insecure and, above all, race-obsessed culture to watch a white German and a dark man stand as one man and his negative reflection and then to watch the dark reflection beat down the German.

Rukeli was not thinking of the psychological attractions or discomforts to his audience. He was training to win and earning steadily. He moved out into his own apartment, in the old city. He bought a fancy hat and a camel hair coat. He went out dancing at the Steuerndied, the Crystall-Palast, the Rote Mühle, and on Sunday afternoons to the Melini-Theater.

He had a girlfriend and on weekends liked to take her out to have lemonade at the Tivoli Gardens, a private park that was crowded on weekends with good weather. People sometimes recognized him. His closest friend at the time was another athlete and local celebrity, the wrestler Max Walloschke. Originally from Breslau, Max had settled and opened a restaurant in Hannover. When without his girl, Rukeli could be found holding court and eating at Max's.

One day he went off his beaten path and tried a new bar. As he sat at the bar and started his drink, a man with a dog, a Boxer took the place next to him. The dog looked up at the Sinto and growled. Rukeli warned that he would knock the dog out if he didn't back off. The owner laughed at the idea that anyone could come out unharmed in a fight with his animal. They made a 20 Mark bet that he could not. They went outside and Rukeli asked the man to go around a corner and then let the dog loose. The Boxer came running. According to the story, Rukeli hit it in the mouth as it was in mid-air, leaping toward him and knocked the animal out. The owner paid his bet.

He was always up for a bet. One Sinto, perhaps jealous at the attention Rukeli drew within the community, said at a large gathering that he could knock Rukeli out. He wagered 20 Marks on it. Trollmann offered a deal. He would let the man hit him four times, at 5 Marks per blow. At the end, Rukeli would be allowed to throw one punch in return. The man accepted and Rukeli stood still while the angry braggart hit him with his best four times. Then Rukeli offered a new deal. Before he would strike back, would the man like to hit him some more? The other man produced ten more Marks and hit him two more times, doing no damage. Rukeli never hit him back. He walked off with the thirty Marks.

On another occasion, Sinti in Berlin organized a party to host Rukeli during his visit to the city. Thought it was the night before a fight, he could not refuse the hospitality. A tent was pitched with food, beer and live music. There were well-dressed girls. Men surrounded Rukeli, all eager to meet Rukeli and to talk about the next day's fight.

One especially large and powerfully built man named Berengo talked angrily and maybe jealously about him from across the tent. "Who is this little sausage?" he demanded.

Rukeli was making his way over in his expensive camel hair coat, shaking hands and moving through the crowd. When he reached Berengo and his friends, Berengo, much larger than the boxer, lifted him up and threw him to the ground. Rukeli banged his head on the earth floor. Anyone who has ever fallen flat at a carnival or raucous party in a tent knows the smell and feel of it. Face down in dirt that so many people have trodden with their dusty shoes, there was a smell of spilled beer or food. The tent went quiet, with only Berengo's voice heard as he continued to insult the guest. Rukeli stood up, slowly dusted himself off and then threw a punch that knocked Berengo out. He would later tell friends that it had been like getting hit with a sledgehammer.

As this was happening, a young woman from a well-educated and established family, Helene Mayer entered her first year at the University of Frankfurt. She aimed to study languages and law and hoped in time to join the German diplomatic corps. In the meantime she was a star athlete. In her first year at the university, she would win the German national women's foil fencing championship for the sixth time. We will have reason to return to Helene Mayer in the years and pages ahead.

It was also at this time that Django Reinhardt sat in a charity hospital near the Gare du Nord in Paris' Tenth Arrondissement. He had come home late at night from a gig and woken his pregnant wife in their caravan. She reached for a match to light a candle, fumbled and started a fire. His wife made it outside. Django was not as quick. When he made it out of the fire, other residents of the caravan site rolled him on the ground and extinguished the flames but not before he had severe burns on much of his body. He lost skin and muscle on his side, on his left hand and on his legs. The injury saved him from military service – a draft enforcer came to his hospital bed to verify the extent of the damage before scratching him for a list – but also took away the use of his two smaller fingers and reduced the dexterity of others. His hand was now more of a hooked claw. He could still use the left thumb to secure a guitar neck. In his hospital bed for months, he designed a new system of playing with new chord forms and practiced with the fingers that remained functional.

For Rukeli, life was a seesaw, training hard in the day and playing with equal fervor when it was time to socialize. In 1931 Rukeli would find it more difficult to book fights. He stepped into the ring just six times that year. This is a recklessly busy schedule for today's top professional fighter but not much for Trollmann. Two of the fights were with Erich Tobeck, the middleweight champion who had beaten him in 1930, and Rukeli continued to lose to him on points.

The next year, on the other hand, he fought nineteen times. Speaking of Ali and the balance between fighting enough to gain experience and the risk of exhaustion, George Foreman once quipped, "I got a dog who fights all the time. He comes home whipped." Rukeli was fighting enough to remember the pain of his whippings. It is hard to imagine him resting enough to get over them. He was simply not one to rest.

It was not only a busy time for Rukeli. In the spring, Hitler had challenged the over-the-hill President Hindenburg, who was running for a second term. Hindenburg won by 19 million votes to Hitler's 13 million.

As Hitler took on the country's top political figure, Rukeli would only go up against the top German fighters in their weight classes. He competed internationally in welter, middle, and half-heavyweight categories. He remained unconcerned with wins or losses. He gained experience and he gained pay.

The best middleweight in Germany was Erich Seelig, who had so recently been Rukeli's own trainer. With his brother Heinrich managing his career, Seelig took the middleweight title in 1932 and then also took the light-heavyweight title in 1933. He was two years younger and a bit more than a pound heavier than Rukeli. He was also Jewish, born in Bomberg (Bydgoszcz in Polish), a city that had changed hands from the German Empire to Poland. The Nazis would eventually invade Poland and bring the city back into German hands. With the help of the Soviets, the city would return to Poland in 1945. At the time of Seelig's birth, Bomberg was 84% German. As a Jewish child with younger brothers to protect, he learned to box and found that he excelled at it. Though educated as an engineer, fighting would be his only profession.

Rukeli had his shot to fight Seelig in Berlin, at the Bockbrauerei in June 1932. Seelig was younger by three years and yet he was the champion and recent teacher, and Trollmann was the upstart. Box-Sport reported on Seelig's match with the "dangerous Gypsy… Seelig was significantly smoother than usual, worked more economically, had more overview."

Two fighters who knew one another, and knew each other's strengths and weaknesses intimately, squared off. Today professional fighters prepare by studying videos of one another's past fights. They are expected to have a strategy that takes into account the other athlete's strengths and weaknesses. In the 1930s, a match-up of two fighters who had the opportunity to think through one another's advantages was not nearly as common.

In the first round Seelig got several hard shots to Rukeli's body and avoided Rukeli's fierce left. In the second round, Rukeli seemed to have things figured out. He kept distance and Seelig was forced to chase him, rarely earning a point. By the third round, however, Rukeli needed to clinch much of the time, as Seelig was better at close range. Seelig was, all the same, forced to work and he took a hard right to the head from Rukeli. Seelig came out of the round having taken some damage but with more points, hitting both body and head. Rukeli won the fourth round and, according to Box-Sport, the crowd.

In the fifth, Seelig dominated, though the round closed with Rukeli delivering a flurry of fists and showing that the fight could still go to either man. As the bell sounded, both were heavily battered. They had butted heads and Seelig had a contusion. Rukeli's lips and both eyes were swollen.

Seelig stayed ahead and took the sixth round. A right to the head dropped Rukeli to the mat. He came up right away, went to the ropes and clinched Seelig tightly. The crowd was back to cheering for Seelig now.

In the seventh, both fighters were tired. The referee, Max Pippow warned Seelig for throwing punches after the bell. In the eight and ninth, Rukeli looked wobbly on his feet. Seelig continued to gain in points. Box-Sport noted a strong uppercut landed by him in the tenth, yet Rukeli took the round. He was not done.

Still, it was too late to catch up. By the end Seelig won on points, more than twice as many as Rukeli landed, and retained his place as the title holder.

Rukeli soon fought again, this time against Walter Sabbotke. Max Schmeling, who had lost the world heavyweight title in Madison Square Garden to Jack Sharkey in a controversial encounter just weeks before[30], was not able to come and sit in the audience but some of his team were there to watch. Rukeli knocked his opponent out in the second round. Box-Sport commented: "...beautiful harmony...it could not have been stronger and more dramatic."

"Sabbotke is out of business after this loss while his conqueror...is even more in it. The Gypsy...danced an imaginative step in the ring..."

The appreciation of his footwork was mixed with less respectful writing. The paper had, for example, taken to referring to him with nicknames. He was called "Heinrich" as often as Johann (*Heini* was common slang for a moron at the time.) and his ethnicity seemed as interesting as his fight style to the writers who covered his career.

In July the Nazis won 230 seats in the Reichstag, the national legislature, more than doubling their power and becoming the largest party. They were in control. They had promised a government committed to the working class. They were, Nazis so often said, a party for the average German. They were for standing up to the big bankers and international financiers. In fact, once in power the Nazis proved that the populist rhetoric was a front for corporate and elite interests. Wages would, in the coming months and years, steadily decline as income from factory ownership and investment rose.[31] The government quickly set up large-scale public infrastructure projects as a way to put people to work. Such jobs, however, were often not as nice as the propaganda claimed. Most men working on the Autobahn, a creation of the Nazi state, earned less than they had been getting in unemployment benefits and were required to live far from home, in barracks where the cost of their shelter and daily soup, ladled out of a cauldron and compared by its consumers to prison fare, were deducted from their pay.

As the facts failed to show that Nazism protected working people from any of the real world exploitation of the rich, the hatred of imaginary villains, especially Jews and racial groups who posed a threat to Germany's greatness, mounted.

Abraham Plotkin was a Jewish American living in Berlin. He found that everywhere he went, Jews had questions about what they might find if they left home. "Do they ever throw Jews out of subway cars in New York?...Do they ever come into stores belonging to Jews and tear up all the stock…?"[32]

Edward Mowrer wrote of Hitler: "He wants to unite all Germans…*Lebensraum* within Central Europe, to install all the regained German subjects…expansion to the east, peaceful or by force, is an inevitable necessity." If the Nazis' ultimate goals were confusing to some, they were very clear to other observers.

Minister of Popular Enlightenment and Propaganda Joseph Goebbels put radio under government control and soon newspapers were also seized. Censorship began, extending from news coverage into the arts. Jazz, despised by the Nazi leadership, was not to be played during state-run radio programs. Minister Goebbels stopped shy of completely outlawing the music form; it was already the rage.

Instead, radio managers were told to stick to European bands and to stay away from music made by Americans and Blacks.

Meanwhile, the Nazis' favorite boxer, Schmeling and his people were impressed with what they had seen of Rukeli. Schmeling had attended several of his fights and the two boxers had become well acquainted. He often gave Rukeli small good luck charms before he fought. His manager offered the young Sinto a chance to go to the United States to fight. Rukeli chose to stay in Europe. He had his parents and siblings in Germany, and by that time in life had several nieces and nephews. He could not imagine leaving them. As Diana says, "Family is everything to us. He could not leave."

In August, he fought the Swedish champion, Karl Ogren who had won twenty-one of his career's twenty-three fights and who had fought Seelig with no decision.

Trollmann beat Ogren on points. Box-Sport was not impressed. "The point victory," the paper editorialized, "must have been very close". The young boxer steamed. A German boxer was winning internationally and the German boxing press, previously willing to praise him, offered only cynicism.

In September, Rukeli fought the Argentine Onofrio Russo in Berlin. "Trollmann's style" said Box-Sport "has returned to his Gypsy ways…Against Russo, who has no legs and only once landed a good hook to the head, he… raced around in an unpredictable manner. In the second round, he hit the Argentinean a couple times on the chin… Russo fell, came up, and was again hit with two hooks that landed more with the underarm than with the gloves… The hits certainly were not correct, but because Trollmann is at the moment the favorite of Berlin, he could get away with such a fighting style. Russo remained lying down and allowed the count,"

Again Trollmann defeated a foreign fighter in October, the Dutch light-heavyweight champion Rienus De Boer. Again the German press berated Trollmann as a Gypsy rather than a proper athlete and showed a clear desire for a white foreigner to win over a Sinto German. "De Boer, who can't have much in the way of brains, fell for Trollmann's tricks and had no trust in himself or his animal power. If Trollmann hit, then De Boer covered, and the Gypsy landed mostly on the arms and elbows…In the eighth round, Trollmann finally tried to use his speed, landed a couple quite well, and took the victory,"

In October, in Dresden Rukeli fought against Josef Czichos. Box-Sport commented that "the Gypsy Trollmann has a lot of attraction" yet treated the appeal as having been poorly earned. The paper criticized his style. It is possible that Rukeli was not exactly the sort of hard-working, humble athlete that sports media would love. He could be proud. Rukeli arrived late to the fight and was slightly overweight – his opponent agreed to fight him all the same and Rukeli was fined 5 Marks for the infraction. Yet the Box-Sport coverage reads as distinctly hostile: "What he did in the ring…had little to do with boxing. Hits with open hands…low blows…were hardly unintentional." The newspaper accused the referee of not dealing harshly enough with Rukeli "even if the public does not agree". This last turn of phrase suggests that Box-Sport's version was not only in dispute with the referee but with the live audience's opinion.

In November Trollmann won again and Box-Sport was displeased as ever. When he fought against Cologne's Hein Domgörgen, Rukeli came out on top and the press remarked: "Domgörgen has gotten older and…Trollmann today was in better condition, yet it remains…that the superiority of the Cologner's infighting was so noticeable the…verdict was not fair…Domgörgen should have won… and it would not have harmed Trollmann's career in the least had he been declared the loser. Because in the end, to be defeated by Domgörgen, if older then still a very good man, means no shame." It is a strange argument. By this logic, Rukeli won the fight but the victory should have been handed to the other fighter because, after all, he was a greater and elder man.

A letter by a writer calling himself Punch may well have been written by Rukeli, or at least a confidant. Noting that the paper had consistently mixed up his name and called him Heinrich, Punch argued, "Trollmann merits being called by his correct name.

Opponents who allow themselves to be forced into his fighting style...have no chance. His style drives form boxers mad. He talks to himself. He uses punches that aren't in any textbook. Bluffs." Unable to make the press stop referring to him as "the Gypsy", Rukeli and his corner began to parody the name with a deliberate dumbing down and chose the nickname *der Gibsy*.

In November he fought against Adolf Witt, a fighter from Kiel who outweighed him by twelve pounds. The fight ended with no decision. They had a rematch in December and this time Witt won on points. Box-Sport was conciliatory, finding that Trollmann "fought bravely" against a larger opponent. Trollmann, it offered, "is to be seen as a great loser". He was more likeable when losing.

Rukeli's nineteen fights in 1932 made him the country's most active professional fighter of the year. Did he chase money rather than focusing on becoming the strongest and best fighter? Whatever his motives, any boxer getting into the ring that often is foregoing the time to train, to rest, to heal injuries. Rukeli was taking fights on short notice against people who were not a good match. He leapt to take up opportunities to earn when others fell sick or dropped out.

This was the year when Ludwig Haymann, boxing fan and Nazi fanatic became the sports editor of the *Völkischer Beobachter*, the Nazi newspaper. Haymann was one of the first and most passionate advocates of the notion that there was a distinctly German (and hence superior) form of pugilism, markedly different from the corrupt sport seen in America and the UK. To keep German athletes fighting the right way, the sport needed to be purified of inferior races. Jews in particular had long diminished "our terms of heroics and idealism", he wrote. "The fight doesn't appeal to the Jews, but rather money...[The Jew] has the capability and the urge to change the sense of any subject to the opposite."

Boxing had become serious sport in Germany. The Nazis would make the study of boxing a compulsory part of all boys' ninth grade education in 1934 and promote the sport in higher education. Already in 1933, they encouraged its practice and used the sport as a recruitment tool. While this attention could mean great prestige and bigger pay for the sort of athletes that the regime favored, it also meant that boxing was under political scrutiny.

The sports editor at the *Völkischen Beobachter* wrote of Trollmann that he did not fight in a German style. "The Gypsy boxes Jewish." Box-Sport picked up the theme, editorializing on the importance of a uniquely German style in opposition to the "cultivated" English form or the "whirlwind, fast-paced close fighting from America". As in many things, the fascist analysis of Rukeli was inconsistent; Box-Sport disapproved of infighting as especially American and yet saw Trollmann, who avoided close range exchanges and liked to think and explore while using footwork, as unacceptable. The hero of German boxing, Max Schmeling was, despite great striking power, also no toe-to-toe brawler but he received very positive reviews.

Schmeling vs. Baer

The changing tide in Germany and the political influence on boxing was impossible for Rukeli's hero and supporter, the twenty-eight year old Max Schmeling to ignore no matter how he tried to focus on his craft. The boxing superstar had risen with a Jewish trainer and manager as well as the support of a social circle full of Jews. According to many accounts he was discovered by Jewish friend Paul Damski, who promoted him in the beginning of his fighting career and even bought him a country house. Aside from the Jews, Schmeling's circle included many artists and intellectuals who the new rulers did not admire. He would be pressed to adapt to the times.

With an eye on international competition, he worked with the New York-based manager Joe Jacobs, known to the press as Yussel the Muscle. Columnist Westbrook Pegler called Jacobs "a New York sidewalk boy of the most conspicuous Jewishness". Jacobs organized a deal for Schmeling to fight Max Baer. The Nazi press called him an "unpleasant, loud-mouthed American Jew" but did not convince Max to dump him. He delivered the Baer fight.

As Schmeling trained, Hitler summoned him to meet. It was the first of several encounters. "If anyone over there asks how it's going in Germany," Hitler instructed him, "you can reassure the doomsayers that everything is moving along quite peacefully."

Fans in Germany and in America waited eagerly for the match and the press worked the story for all it was worth. Germans wanted to see how German boxing trumped the corrupt, money-polluted American sport. Americans wanted to see a Nazi hero go down. "There are many Hebrews here and they are bitter against Hitler and confuse every German with the Nazis, which is tough for Schmeling," Jacobs told a Montreal paper. "He is not a Nazi…not at all in sympathy with their propaganda." He went on that Schmeling would box free for Jewish charities (He never did so.) and that he had even attended synagogue with Jacobs.

Schmeling, however, still lived in Germany and had no intent of emigrating. This required a balancing act. Unlike the "loud-mouthed" Jacobs, Schmeling did not live in a free country and had to be careful in expressing political and racial views. He never joined the Nazi party but, when asked by press about "conditions in Germany", he slipped and ducked:

"What conditions?"

"The political situation."

"I don't know anything about politics."

He was with Jacobs in Maine when they learned of the ban on Jews in boxing. Reporters sought him out. No comment.

As much as he tried to avoid criticizing his government, he repeatedly voiced a belief in equality. Questioned by one German journalist about racial differences among boxers, he said: "For me, there exists no racial dividing line in sports." This was not towing the line.

As the public on both sides of the Atlantic made Schmeling into a Nazi despite his own sentiments, Baer also found himself the object of public and media imagination. Baer was a quarter Jewish but had no Jewish community, cultural or religious ties. When the press started to identify him as a Jew, he went with it. It made for good fight promotion and made him attractive to the Jewish fans. Trainer Ray Arcel years later said he had seen him in showers and could "confirm without doubt" that Baer was *not* Jewish. Whether Baer was the fake that Arcel and many others later claimed, the identification with Jewry was new for Baer when the fight's promotion began.

"Every punch in the eye I give Schmeling is one for Adolf Hitler," said Baer. Going into the ring on the night of fight, he wore trunks with a Star of David. It was his first but not last time doing so.

Baer knocked Schmeling down in the tenth after a difficult match. Returning to the dressing room, he looked at his badly swollen nose in a mirror. "They thought I was a Hebe and now I look like one."

Insofar as Baer's Jewish identity was an act, Germany bought it and the German government was not pleased at his success. A comedy film in which he starred, *The Prizefighter and the Lady* was censored. "They didn't ban the picture because I have Jewish blood," commented Baer. "They banned it because I knocked out Max Schmeling."

After the fight, the German press mostly ignored him and studiously avoided reporting Schmeling's loss. Instead, Schmeling coverage focused on his recent engagement to Anny Ondra. A Polish-born, ethnically Czech actress, she had played small roles in Hitchcock films. When Schmeling and Ondra married, Hitler sent a wedding gift.

When the U.S. eventually declared war on Germany, Max Baer quickly enlisted, as did many boxers.

Trollmann's Title Shot

In February 1933, Rukeli fought the Afro-Carribbean boxer Claude Bassin for the second time. They had fought first in 1932 and Bassin had knocked Trollmann out. The second fight ended in a *no decision* to the dismay of Box-Sport. The report of the fight argued that Bassin should have won and went on to explain why the newspaper would stand in favor of a Black athlete, the *"Cuba-Neger Bassin"*: "Because they [Black athletes] generally bring, compared to good boxing traits...so many bad ones of their black race to the ring... this black man Bassin, who can be presented as the fairest, most respectable boxing black that has appeared in Germany".

That same month Box-Sport explained the new racial policy, or Aryanization of the sport. Jews were no longer permitted to participate in any way. Not only would Jews no longer compete as athletes, they were henceforth cast out of any role. Trainers and managers needed to be Aryan. Jewish doctors were not even to treat Aryan boxers as patients. Cut men, the men who counted the points and the announcers were all no longer welcome. The head of the new Nazi-established national boxing association, Georg Radamm declared: "Adolf Hitler has promoted boxing but not for the individual, as the corrupt Jewish exploiters think...rather for a movement that binds true German young men to the community of the Volk [nation]."

Beyond boxing, it was determined that only Aryans could join the German Turnerschaft, a students' sports fraternal organization. The government forced the Workers Sport Clubs to close, seeing them as intolerably Marxist. Their facilities were nationalized and handed over to Hitler Youth and SS units.

Hitler's views about inter-racial sports competition are easy to understand if one recalls his own early experiences in politics. In prison in 1924, he began to gain weight thanks to gifts of food and wine from outside well wishers. A visitor, noting that Hitler had quickly put on eleven pounds (reaching a weight of one hundred seventy), advised him to take part in some of the prison's sport activities. "It would be bad for discipline if I took part in physical training," the young revolutionary explained. "A leader cannot afford to be beaten at games."[33] What is true for the individual must have been true for the leading race.

Rukeli and his manager, Zirzow had been trying to set up a title fight, a new match against the champion Erich Seelig. Seelig, Rukeli's old trainer had simultaneously held the middle and light-heavyweight national belts. Now Seelig would be forced to abandon his profession and his titles. Hitler himself had attended a Seelig fight and his quick removal from the sport was given high importance. Seelig received an official letter in July, on the eve of a fight to defend his middleweight tile, warning him not to compete[34] and giving him two weeks to leave the country. When his time was up, he was escorted to the airport – according to the version told years later to his family – with a gun to his head in the car. He was told that both he and his family would die if he returned. Seelig went to France, where he competed and won five of seven matches before he was again forced to flee the invading Nazis. He had, luckily, earned and saved enough by then for travel to Cuba. From there, he fought again and won until he earned enough to pay the way for his mother, four brothers and sister to go with him to the United States. There too he would box.

Fighting in America was not initially pleasant for Seelig. In one early fight, the crowd at Madison Square Garden booed him. It had been announced that he was from Germany and the fans began to shout insults at what they assumed to be a Nazi. He learned his lesson and would henceforth fight in shorts with a Star of David on the left leg. He built a record of 57 pro fights in America, rising to the rank of #6 in *The Ring* magazine in 1938. It was also in America that he would eventually meet his wife, Greta. She too fled Germany after her Jewish racial background made her ineligible to compete in the hurdles in the 1936 Olympics.

As Seelig left, Trollmann defeated Fred Bölck. Rukeli took to fighting monthly. Perhaps he knew that it would not be long before the race policy included him too. Every fight could be his last. In March, he fought Helmut Hartkopp in Hamburg's Flora Theater.

In April, Schniplo passed away. Rukeli's training was interrupted by mourning. Nonetheless, he fought Hans Siefried. Seeing that Trollmann could not be taken on points, Siefried struggled to land heavy blows and to get a knock out. There was no chance. In the final round, Rukeli was going strong and landed a powerful hook to Siefried's body. The audience booed the referee when a no decision was announced.

It was May when Joseph Goebbels planned with the national student association and presided over the highly publicized "burning of the books". At universities across the country, books considered un-German were thrown into the fires. Books by German writers such as Remarque and Brecht (and, of course, Marx and Engels) burned along with the works of Sigmund Freud, Ernest Hemingway, H.G. Wells, Jack London and the renowned socialist Helen Keller. Keller replied to German students in an open letter, urging them to note whose work they burnt: "I gave all my royalties of my books for all time to the German soldiers blinded in the World War with no thought in my heart but love and compassion for the German people".

A week later Trollmann fought in Amsterdam against Gustave Roth, the Belgian and European welterweight champion. Rukeli lost by a few points, earning praise in the Belgian press but not at home.

And only ten days after the Amsterdam encounter, no doubt still bruised, he laced up his gloves to fight Otto Klockemann at home in Hannover. Klockemann was fifteen pounds heavier than Rukeli. Again, any fight against any opponent. The fight was at the Konzerthaus and friends were there to see it. The Trollmann family sat ringside and the crowd cheered as Rukeli jumped over the ropes into the ring. He knocked Klockemann to the mat in the second round and the hometown crowd went wild seeing the local boy drop a larger fighter.

Celebrating, Rukeli carried his sister Kerscha's eight-year-old daughter into the ring. SA members shouted that there should be no more Gypsies in the ring.

Seelig's title sat in the open and waited for someone to claim it. At last, Trollmann was scheduled to fight with Adolf Witt.

As the fight approached, Box-Sport said that Kiel's Witt and Hannover's Trollmann each were "magnets" with their own followers. "…Witt, people come to see a strong, brave and always a dangerous puncher…." Trollmann fans, however, it was argued, "value the theatrical in his style, the Gypsy unpredictability… It can also be that Trollmann's talents can be steered to very different ends…" Even in the boxing ring, one had to worry whether successful ethnic minorities were plotting to apply their assets in dark ways. Again the newspaper said that his "Gypsy demonstrations… have little in common with boxing".

Repplinger points out that *Box-Sport*, most ominously of all, wrote at this point of Witt in the present tense and often switched to the past when describing Rukeli. It was as if the boxing press was offering an obituary.

The fight was held in the open air on June 9th at Berlin's Bockbierbrauerei, a giant beer hall where a variety of events were convened in the Kreuzberg area. Shortly before the event, a storm seemed to be looming and only 1,500 people ventured out to watch. It not an impressive showing for a title fight. People took their seats and baked good vendors stalked through the rows of seating. As always, Rukeli was the smaller and lighter boxer. Box-Sport did not approve of letting him have a shot at the title. "The Gypsy is a feeling fighter, an instinct boxer who, with his jumping around, often strays from the sports line. Often…one can look away and not denounce the un-seriousness of his boxing. When it is about the official title, then there is the danger that the intrinsic value of a title can be lessened…"

Witt won the first round. He was kept down the rest of it. Rukeli scored repeatedly with his left. Witt tried to go for solid blows but found Rukeli's footwork and defensive style hard to pin down. Witt was hitting nothing. With a larger live audience (presumably including soldiers) and national press to observe, hard facts dispelled paperbound theories of the superiority of the Aryan character.

Georg Radamm, who oversaw the national boxing association was in the stands and, in the sixth round, whispered to the referee. There was nothing to be done. With Rukeli clearly ahead on points, those who did not want him to win would have to wait and hope for Witt to put him down. Witt, meanwhile, worked in vain.

The bell sounded at the end of the twelfth and final round. The crowd was silent as the referee took the center of the ring. "No decision". The title would stay open. Both fighters stood motionless and said nothing. Zirzow too froze.

It was only when the crowd came to life, shouting and jumping from their seats that Zirzow went into motion. He cursed, ran around the ring and made threats. He grabbed the judges' scorecards and showed them to anyone who would look. Rukeli had won on points.

As fights broke out in the stands and Zirzow stood in the ring, egging the crowd on by waving the scorecards in the air, Trollmann moved to the dressing room. He sat down, exhausted and cried. Training and beating the opponent was not enough. Zirzow fetched him and pushed him to return to the ring, to see the crowd's support. As Box-Sport put it, "Zirzow, the manager of Trollmann whizzed like a small rocket around the ring, spoke with twitching lips, was one minute here, one minute there, maltreated tables with his fists and appeared suddenly with the crying Trollmann, who he brought back from the dressing room".

Radamm and the promoters came to stand together before the audience. They announced that they would take a look at the scorecards. They made a show of examining the numbers. Yes, there had been an error.

Trollmann was declared the winner and the new light-heavyweight champion. He was the champion of his sport in the country that viewed itself as Europe's and the world's strongest nation. He was the top in a weight class whose victors would later include such American stars as Archie Moore, Cassius Clay (later Mohammed Ali) and Evander Holyfield. The crowd rejoiced. Rukeli was elated.

On the next business day, a Monday, the boxing authority met. Hearing from the referee, Radamm and party officials, the official body nullified the result: "In the fight of Heinrich *(sic)* Trollmann-Adolf Witt on 9 June in the Bockbierbrauerei, regarding the title of German champion in the light-heavyweight class, [the result] is canceled and the fight, because of the insufficient effort of both fighters, is…a fight without a decision". Zirzow and the other troublemakers were fined for disputing with the referee.

Adolf Witt went on to win the title in 1933 and hold it until 1937.

In July, Rukeli would fight again, dropping enough weight to move down and compete as a welterweight against the welterweight title-holder from Dortmund, a boxer named Gustav "Eisener" (iron) Eder. Eder was shorter and lighter, even after Rukeli's rapid weight loss.

The people who bought tickets for the fight had no idea of the show Trollmann was planning to give them. He had been warned by the boxing authorities to fight in the correct "German style". And so, if he could not fight his own game, he came up with another approach.

When the boxers were called to the ring, Rukeli entered with hair dyed a shocking blond. He was wet and covered from head to toe in white powder. By some accounts and family lore, he used flour. In other versions, it was stage make-up.

He had not only made the effort through stage make-up to look like a white German. He fought as the people in charge said an Aryan should. From the first round, he hardly budged his feet. He stood and dared Eder to come and exchange blows, foot to foot with no retreat. It is hard to see whether the writers at Box-Sport understood the meaning what they were watching. The paper reported tersely: "Trollmann gave it his all and really came as a fighter in the ring". It also noted without fuss that he had lightened his hair.

Eder got away with a low blow before landing "a murderous right to the solar-which drew large numbers of whistles" from the crowd.

Even with Rukeli staying more or less rooted in place and even with a bit of cheating, Iron Eder had trouble. By the end of the second round, Eder was bleeding badly. In the third, Rukeli backed him into a corner and pounded on him. There was one noted shot to Rukeli's middle. Otherwise, Trollmann dominated the round.

In the fourth, Eder knocked Rukeli off his feet twice. The second time, he stayed down and steadied himself until the count of nine, then jumped up to deliver an uppercut. Rukeli was knocked down and came back up again.

Rukeli's cut man was unable to stop the bleeding between rounds. The powder was becoming a mess.

In the fifth, Rukeli had had enough of the slugging it out. He went back to boxing, moving his feet. It was too late. He was tired. Two headshots, two to the body and Rukeli fell. He was counted out.

Before Rukeli's decision to use the small, confining ring as a platform for a grand statement that would be heard for generations and long after his departure, Roma and Sinti have struggled with how to engage in protest and how to open the majority's eyes to the experience of exclusion. How does one grab the majority's attention without playing into the stereotypes of the Gypsy performer? As Romani American professor Ethel Brooks wonders, in a discussion of Trollmann, about her own interaction with the Holocaust education establishment: "Do we…want to be the white people's Gypsy? And how do we work without doing that?" Trollmann instinctively cracked the code like few since.

And yet he, as a boxer who trained, sweated and bled in order to win, was knocked out. One can imagine him feeling that there was nothing more to prove, nothing left to win in the ring. What choices did he have? This was Johann Trollmann's profession if not still tied to his entire sense of identity. Walking away from boxing was not an option. There is an old Romani saying for doing what one knows is dangerous because the alternative is even worse. It is "holding the wolf by the ears". Rukeli, it seems, had few pleasant alternatives to holding on tightly.

He fought Sabbotke again in September. For all that he had been through, he had the frame of mind and will to fight and to give his all.

Trollmann, whom Box-Sport now tauntingly called the "ex-Gypsy" in reference to his new hair color, started the fight in his usual form. From the start through the fifth round, he was dominating. Sabbotke at one point scored a hard left and sent Rukeli to the mat in his corner. Rukeli stood and moved along the ropes to get away. It seemed for a moment that Sabbotke had him. And then he let his hands go. The crowd stood on their seats and yelled. Sabbotke was pinned to the ropes until the bell sounded. Rukeli would be on top for the next few rounds.

Was Rukeli really the same man that he had been? He had the spirit to get into the ring and fight. To be a professional fist fighter is not an easy thing, not for the emotionally downtrodden. If he was emotionally crushed by the way the authorities had robbed him, one should note that Rukeli, dominating the fight, spent the rest of it in a brawl, an exchange of hard shots. Yet this was not the same sharp, defensive boxer whose style had been called Gypsy and even Jewish. He was defeated in the sense that he had compromised and abandoned his style. Reading press reports of the fight, it seems like winning may not have been the only thing on his mind. He may have wanted to fight the right way, someone else's way and to be granted approval as much as he fought for anything else.

Unfortunately, fighting someone else's game and style was not how he would win. At the end, a bloody Sabbotke joined him in the center of the ring to await the decision. The crowd applauded both fighters. Box-Sport reported the audience gave them both "an ovation as has not been heard in the Berlin ring in a long time. For his brave fight, the judge gave Sabbotke a no decision, which the public did not agree with."

Later in September, Box-Sport acknowledged Trollmann and Fred Bölck of Hamburg as the official challengers of Hein Domgörgen for the middleweight title.

It was clear that the boxing authority would never let a Gypsy hold the middleweight national title but there was no retiring from the game. According to Repplinger, Rukeli scheduled the fight and the paycheck for October but did not seriously train for it. He was knocked out in the second round.

Later in the month he lost again, to Franz Boja. He approached the ring in a borrowed Sturmabteilung uniform, his hair still blond. His very arrival to the ring made a statement that no other Gypsy in Germany was making, even without uniform and pomp. He did not just go into the ring and lie down. Box-Sport reported that he "ran, danced, fought, and bluffed… and the public applauded for the grotesque entertainment". Maybe there was something to be won after all, something other than a title or a boxing match.

In November, the Flora Theater in Hamburg hosted the Domgörgen-Bölck middleweight championship. Rukeli was there as a closing act, fighting and defeating Gustav Eybel. Box-Sport was less interested in his fighting than the audience's insults. For the newspaper, the most important message to convey to the readers was that German fight fans wanted no Gypsy in their German boxing rings.

"Lie down, Trollmann…or we'll arrest you!" someone shouted.

"Gypsy pig, run off to Wallachia [Romania]!"

He was not there to win but to be vilified.

On November 25, he lost to Erwin Bruch in the second round. Box-Sport wondered whether he had even trained.

He fought Sabbotke again, in December in Hamburg. Sabbotke won on points. Even Box-Sport reported that Trollmann seemed to be goofing around and focused on something other than a win.

It also seems that many fighters understood that Rukeli was through. They lined up to fight against him, to get an easy win on their records.

When he at last stopped fighting, Rukeli's record would be 62 fights. Only thirty were victories, of which an impressive 30 were knockouts. There were 13 no decisions.
He only stopped going to lose when the offers stopped coming and Zirzow was done with him. In January 1934, they dissolved their contract.

To keep earning, Rukeli took fights in Hannover at the Pötte-Markt. These were not sanctioned events and he would lose his boxer's license if the boxing authority found out. And how would they not find out? Still, he had to make a living.

In May, due to these unsanctioned bouts, his license was indeed revoked. With no other skills, he was conscripted to public work service, first shoveling coal and then cleaning planes at Vahrenheide airport. Taking the minimal pay, he simultaneously collected unemployment and bartended some nights in the Old Town. There may be no worse place for a known boxer (or even one whose looks, whose physique and cauliflower ears give him away as a boxer) to work than in a bar. There is always the drinker who wants to test himself against and start a fight. Rukeli was in no position to be picky about how he earned.

Survival: 1934-1936

Sinti were beginning to disappear from Hannover and from Germany. Some exceptional cases came back, emaciated and not keen to talk about what had happened to them. Most did not return.

Rukeli was among the many who feared staying at their official, registered addresses and who took to living on the go. He spent months with other Sinti traveling through the Teutoburg Forest near Bruchhausen-Vilsen. He went by motorcycle to Berlin and stayed for a time with his girlfriend, a domestic servant named Olga Bilda. Like many of the girls he had pursued in the past, she was an eye-catching blond. She would soon enough reveal that the hair was dyed and that she was a brunette. No matter. By then, she proved that she could be more to him than another pretty face looking for fun. They would go a few times to Hannover and stayed a couple days in familiar territory from childhood, the Tiefenthal. Olga won the family over, buying fabrics and sewing for his nieces. She made them dresses with flowery patterns and sequins and the girls, like Rukeli, fawned over her.

In March of 1935 Rukeli and Olga had a daughter, Rita Edith. Olga was nineteen.

Rukeli married her in June at the Berlin-Charlottenburg registration office and they lived together, watching their swaddled baby with awe and with worry. What future lay ahead for a Sinti child?

How could they even send their child to school? Race theories were taught in schools now from the age of six. *Rassenkund*e, or racial knowledge was inserted in all classes, from biology to history. In math class, children were asked how many marriage loans could be paid out to Aryan couples at 1,000 Marks each if the country's 300,000 mentally disabled people in the public care system were eliminated. All teachers were required to join the Nazi Teachers' Association and to attend political education classes.

The Nuremberg racial laws were passed on September 15, 1935. Boxing star Max Schmeling was a celebrity guest at the Nazis' annual congress in Nuremberg just before the laws were announced. It is unknown whether he overheard anything about the policies that were being approved between the hand shaking and photo taking that was expected of him.

The new codes prescribed the complete disenfranchisement of people of "alien blood". The Law for the Protection of German Blood and German Honor forbade marriages and extramarital intercourse between Jews and Germans, as well as the employment of German females under 45 in Jewish households. The Reich Citizenship Law declared that only those of German "or related" blood were eligible to be Reich citizens. Jews were no longer citizens but rather state subjects. The laws were expanded on the 26th of November to explicitly include Roma and Sinti. A ban on intermarriage was intended to stop the spread of inferior genes into the German Aryan gene pool. Those who married across racial lines were exposed to possible criminal prosecution.

Journalist Quentin Reynolds and the US Ambassador's daughter, Martha Dodd were travelling with a group of American officials in Nuremberg. Arriving at their hotel, they found a crowd gathering and asked at the reception if there was a parade planned. The receptionist laughed. "It will be a kind of parade," he said.[35] The Americans went into the street and found people enjoying themselves. There was a Storm Trooper marching band. Two Troopers were dragging a woman down the street with a sign around her neck. It read, "I wanted to live with a Jew." She had been engaged to a Jew, defying the new ban on mixed marriage. The new laws were popular if this very illustrative moment in Nuremburg is representative of the mood in other cities.

The Third Reich had begun policies, though not without precedent in German history, to finally ethnically cleanse the country of all Romani and Sinti people. While Hitler and the Nazi party gave Gypsies less thought than Jews – Hitler barely mentioned them in speeches or writing – they were soon to be marked for genocide in all of Europe, to be exterminated as an inferior race.

The Gypsy Office of the City of Hannover contacted members of the community, including many men in the Trollman family with a choice: sterilization or internment in a concentration camp. Some family members turned themselves in for sterilization. The procedure lasted three day, after which Sinti "patients" left the hospital to recover on their own. By the end of World War Two, ten percent of German Sinti and Roma were sterilized.[36] Many who went through the procedure were nonetheless later sent to camps.

Rukeli's brother Mauso, whose legal name was Julius and their brother Albert were sent to the Rethen Work Camp. Mauso was beaten for talking with his brother during a work break and would die, a few years after the war in a hospital in Langenhagen, from the permanent damage.

Rukeli's younger brother Stabeli, the violin player could no longer find work. Sinti and Roma were no longer hired. His life would end, at the age of twenty-six, in the Auschwitz-Birkenau Concentration Camp, in November 1943 after members of the SS shoved him into a rain barrel and left him there. We will return to Auschwitz-Birkenau.

In September of 1938, the marriage of Olga and Johann Trollmann was ended in divorce in Berlin. By divorcing, Rukeli hoped to separate his family from the laws against Gypsies. Perhaps Olga could benefit from his leaving. His child, of course, was already on record as being half Gypsy. There was little Rukeli could do to cleanse her of this crime.

As noted, the Nazi policy was that the Gypsies in Germany endangered the purity of German blood and thus the survival of the Aryan race. Whereas Nazi efforts to remove Jews from society started with those seen as "full blooded", Nazi attention to Roma and Sinti put the earliest focus on mixed race people (*Mischlinge*). Those who the Nazis determined as pure blooded (*reinrassig*) were often not approached by authorities in the first phase. When the Nazis first took power, Germany was officially home to 13,000 Sinti and 1,585 Roma. Many Sinti had lived in one region or town of Germany for centuries. Some were well integrated into their communities. By Nazi logic, this sort of Gypsy posed the greatest genetic threat.

Dr. Robert Ritter was the researcher behind much of Nazi thinking on Gypsies. He had graduated in Munich in 1927 with a degree in psychology and in 1930 obtained a degree in medicine in Heidelberg. During his studies, Ritter learned from, and looked up to Emil Kraepelin, an influential scientist who found mental illness to be in many cases inherited. Ritter became a leader among many Germany scientists who conducted research in the 1930s on Gypsies and especially on *Zigeunerbastarden*, Gypsy bastards or mongrels. For Ritter and his peers, failures to integrate economically or otherwise into German society were due to genetic inferiority.

In 1936, Ritter was called to the Racial-Hygienic and Genetic Biological Research Center in Berlin-Dahlem, a center funded mainly by the Ministry of the Interior. A year later, he was the Center's director. By 1936, he had records of every Roma and Sinti in Germany, carefully noting whether each person was full, half, a quarter Gypsy and so on, down to one sixteenth. A mixed race Gypsy was someone who had only three or fewer Gypsy grandparents. For the purposes of defining who was Gypsy, having a mixed race Gypsy in one's family tree was enough.

Among the Trollmanns and their cousins, the Weiss family, intermarriage had long been common. Under the policy that would develop, those who integrated fully into German society, attaining an education and a profession and eventually marrying outside the community were to be sterilized and prevented from passing their dangerous blood along. Those who engaged in traditional occupations or those who did itinerant, travelling labor and married within their ethnic communities were "asocial" and criminals.

The first Gypsies rounded up by the police to be sent to concentration camps were 18,000 people of mixed background.

On the basis of "Deportation Decrees" in Bavaria, four hundred Gypsies were arrested in 1936 and brought to the Dachau concentration camp. Because of the 1936 Olympics in Berlin, the

Gypsy Camp Marzahn was created in the east of Berlin Gypsies were brought there so that their presence among good, white Germans would not negatively influence visitors' impressions of the city. Hitler commissioned a statue of Max Schmeling to be placed at the sports facility in Berlin where the Games were to be held.

Before Hitler came to power, he had called the Olympics "an invention of Jews and Freemasons, a ploy inspired by Judaism"[37]. As the leader of a nation with worldwide aspirations, however, he came to see that international sports had propaganda value. Berlin would put on the best and most Aryan face.

As other cities began to move them to concentration sites, the Sinti and Roma were no longer allowed to leave Germany. They were neither welcome in their own country nor free to leave.

The 1936 Olympics

Rukeli had no opportunity to participate in the Olympics. Yet there was no looking away from the Berlin Games. They were the center of the sports world and the German politics of sport from which Rukeli could not escape. A look at how a few other athletes and public figures grappled with the race politics of the time, especially the one Jew who competed on Germany's behalf, reminds us of how unusual Rukeli's view of his own inherent equality truly was.

When the International Olympic Committee met in Barcelona in 1931 and awarded the 1936 Games to Berlin, the competition was put in the hands of a democratic nation.

When Berlin hosted the 1936 Olympics, much had changed. The city's Gypsies were rounded up and removed in order to show the world an Aryan city. Germany had already excluded non-Aryans from sports for years. Erich Seelig and Johann Trollmann had been purged from the top of boxing. Then later, minorities had been denied participation of any kind in all sports.

Berlin had been embarrassed in March of that year when rigged elections gave the Nazis exactly 99% of the vote in each and every district. Now it was time to bury the awkward memory under a global public relations masterpiece. Germany would make Berlin a perfect display, a well-governed showcase city.

Some minority athletes in the lands threatened by Germany wanted nothing to do with the Nazi-hijacked Games. The Jewish Dutch boxer Bennie Bril, like many individual Dutch athletes, chose to boycott the Olympic Games. In Austria, where public pools forbade the entry of dogs and Jews, the Jewish champion swimmer Ruth Langer also refused to go to Berlin.

For as long as Berlin had been planning the Games, Americans had been debating whether to boycott them. Jewish community organizers in New York led the call.

Germany countered at first by stating, despite having already removed all minorities from sports, that German sportsmen of non-Aryan origin *would* be part of their country's representation at the Games, *assuming they qualified*. Yet none were selected in an initial swearing in, held in 1935. One would have to be both an exceptional athlete and a German citizen to qualify. Jews and Gypsies were no longer German citizens when the Nuremberg Laws passed.

Among the American press there were advocates for a boycott, including popular syndicated columnists Heyward Broun and Westbrook Pegler. A Gallup poll in 1935 found that 43% of Americans favored a boycott. (Less than 2% of Americans were Jewish.) President Roosevelt stayed cautiously silent.

Helene Mayer, the star of German women's fencing had won Olympic gold for her country as a teen. She had met leading figures in German politics and high society and been a media darling. Her looks – she was tall, blue-eyed, blonde and well built – received enthusiastic attention and commentary. She was also half Jewish. Her family was not religious and her ethnic background did not play much of a role in her upbringing. Like many of Germany's Jews, who were not more than one percent of the national population, she was not much different from her neighbors. This did not make her background irrelevant. A newspaper article reported that she was known around her neighborhood as Jewish Mayer, to distinguish her from the gentile Mayer girl who lived on the same street. Why not Mayer the fencer, or tall Mayer (she was 5'10"), or one of a hundred other monikers?

In 1932, as politics made life increasingly stressful for everyone in Germany, Helene Mayer joined the Olympic team as a fencer and went to Los Angeles to prepare for the Games. While there, she received a two-year scholarship to Scripps College in Claremont, California. She wanted to perfect her English and have her first experience with life abroad, with the dream of serving in the German diplomatic corps. She arrived on campus as an Olympic athlete and something of a celebrity at a small school. She founded a fencing program there as well as becoming president of the Franco-German Club, the school's most popular student association.

During her first year at Scripps, Hitler would use a fire at the Reichstag as cause to pass an emergency decree that suspended fundamental rights. Dutch communist Marinus van der Lubbe was hastily tried and executed. He was the first of approximately 12,000 civilians who were eventually eliminated by special courts under the Third Reich. In 1933, Jewish businesses were boycotted on a national basis. Sterilization of the disabled began. Blind, deaf and other Germans were put to death upon the orders of public doctors. Helene, whatever she knew of these issues, did not speak of politics according to fellow students. When she spoke of Germany, it was in the most glowing terms.

Three months after the regime change, her membership at the Offenbach Fencing Club, an organization she had made nationally famous, was terminated due to new race laws. In June, a few days after winning the U.S. fencing championship, her exchange fellowship was rescinded on racial grounds. Scripps picked up the bill..

She graduated in 1934 with no hope of fulfilling her professional goal of public service in the German Foreign Ministry. Mills College, not far from Scripps, took her on as a German teacher and fencing coach.

She won the U.S. National Championship for women's foil again, in New York and commented to a reporter that she would "consider it an honor" if Germany would ask her to compete for her country in the 1936 Olympics. Perhaps she was unable to bend her mind around the law that forbade Jews from all sports competition in Germany. Or perhaps she thought that as a half-Jew and a star athlete, she might be exempt.

And she was not all wrong, as things would develop, to hold on to hope. At least, she was not wrong to hope in regard to participating in the Olympics. By 1935, the American Olympic Committee was intensely pressuring Germany to admit at least one Jew to its Olympic representation if the U.S. were to take part in the Games.

Needing to take just one Jew to satisfy American concerns and avoid a boycott, Germany settled on inviting Helene Mayer – whose citizenship had been stripped – to compete for her former country. As Heyward Broun observed, it was "bitter irony to say…We hold you inferior, but that would not prevent us from using your superiority temporarily as an asset to the German team."

Mayer, aching to compete in the Games, proudly accepted her place even though it was the result of international coercion.

In November 1935, she complicated matters by attaching a demand to her participation; she would compete only if her citizenship was restored. This, it should be clear, was not a protest of the Nuremberg Laws but an appeal to be exempted from them. She met with the German Consul General in San Francisco and he agreed to make an effort on her behalf. The Nuremberg Laws defined a mixed Jew as having at least two Jewish grandparents and belonging to a Jewish religious community. Mayer had the former but not the latter. Consul General Hinrich appealed to the German Embassy in Washington, D.C.

After much lobbying and press attention, the German Olympic Committee assured her that her demand could be met. What exactly happened, however, is unclear. According to some Polish media reports, Helene regained her citizenship by signing a statement that she had no blood relation to her Jewish father, claiming to be the product instead of her Aryan mother and an extramarital partner. According to other sources, German government tests had found that Helene was not really half Jewish but only a quarter and therefore eligible. However she was taken onto the team, she made no commotion on behalf of other athletes or other Jews whose opportunities were taken away. She did not challenge anti-Semitic policy other than by denying that it pertained to *her*.

As she prepared for the Games, Germany expelled Jewish children – even half Jews like her and even if they were baptized Christians– from public schools. She made no remark and there is no indication that she felt doubts about whether this was a country for which she still wished to compete.

The opening of the Olympics was feted with clouds and the threat of storms, yet crowds filled the stadium. The Hindenburg zeppelin floated overhead with swastikas on its tails and pulling an Olympic flag behind it.

The Roma and Sinti of the city had been evicted. Jews, not allowed to fly the swastika, hung Olympic flags from apartment windows. Anti-Semitic signs and posters were taken down. The government planned to make fools out of the foreigners who said things were so bad for minorities here. In general, censorship was lifted in the city for the Games. American jazz was temporarily allowed in bars.

The boxing matches, like fencing and wrestling, were to be held at the grand Germany Hall on the Konigsweg, one of the city's main roads.

Children played with collectible cards of their favorite Olympic team members, produced by German cigarette companies.

Hitler arrived to the Games in the afternoon with Olympic officials in frocks and top hats at his sides, followed by his friends. There was the king of Bulgaria, the princes of Italy, Greece and Sweden and the sons of the Italian dictator, Mussolini. A military band played a march by Richard Strauss.

American author Thomas Wolfe was there to see it: "At last he [Hitler] came...a little dark man with a comic-opera mustache, erect and standing, moveless and unsmiling, with his hand upraised, palm outward, not in Nazi-wise salute but straight up in a gesture of blessing such as the Buddha or Messiah use."

The crowds saluted with the *Sieg Heil,* as did the foreign athletes. Only the American athletes held their banners upright as their host passed, drawing whistles and shouts from the crowd. Nazi press later smoothed the matter over, explaining that no disrespect was intended and that US regulations did not allow the flag to be lowered for anyone but the US president.

In the women's foil fencing, Helene Mayer and two other competitors, from Austria and Hungary, had a draw. On points, a Hungarian Jew, Ilona Schacherer-Elek took the gold. Helene, who had come so close, wept.

As a finalist, she would stand in front of the throng of spectators once more. She took her place next to the winner and other runner up, wearing her assigned white turtleneck that she adorned with a swastika pin. The crowd applauded as she gave the Heil Hitler salute. Her negotiated citizenship never came through.

Hitler watched the Games and applauded the German winners in an "orgiastic frenzy of shrieks, clappings, and contortions"[38] but showed disinterest or worse when others won. He was especially unhappy about Jesse Owens, whom he watched with Schmeling and other special guests by his side. "It was unfair of the United States to send these flatfooted specimens to compete with the noble products of Germany," complained Hitler. "I am going to vote against Negro participation in the future."

Not all Germans were so inhospitable to the runner. Owens was visited in the Olympic village by the founder of the Adidas athletic shoe company and accepted a gift of shoes. W.E.B. DuBois spent a half-year on a fellowship in Germany in 1935-36 and wrote: "Jesse Owens ran before the astonished eyes of the world. He was lauded and pictured and interviewed…And while Hitler and other top Nazis bitterly complained about the African American Olympians, some of those athletes were invited by ordinary German citizens for coffee or dinner." As for himself, he wrote, "I have been treated with uniform courtesy." He noted the "campaign of race prejudice carried on…against all non-Nordic races, but specifically against the Jews, which surpasses in vindictive cruelty and public insult anything I have ever seen".

Considering that African Americans experienced considerable discrimination and mistreatment at home, it is easier to understand why some who visited Germany with honored status and certain privileges did not focus on Germany's domestic race policies. It was not a primary concern that Nazism saw jazz as "nigger music". They may not even have been aware of how Germany was treating its own approximately 25,000 Blacks. Those who knew perhaps were not shocked. While the Nuremberg Laws had taken away Blacks' citizenship and forbidden marriage with whites, intermarriage was also illegal in parts of the U.S. It is at times written that the Nazi regime sterilized Afro-Germans; this is only partly true. It is the case of a total of about 500 young people who were the result of mixed marriages between German women and Afro-French occupying soldiers after World War I, the so-called "Rhineland Bastards". It was not a policy affecting all Afro-Germans. Blacks were still welcome at German universities in 1936, unlike in much of the U.S.

Whatever African Americans thought about Nazi race policies, Jesse Owens made no public statements on the issue.

Germany won more medals at the Berlin Olympics than all other countries combined, including the United States. In boxing, an African-American won a silver medal but Germany took two medals. In Rukeli's weight class, the gold went to a French fighter.

Hitler was quite pleased with Germany's overall success. The achievements of Negro individuals like Owens, as well as the 13 medals won by Jews from various countries were buried under the German press coverage of German medals.

Two days after the closing ceremony, the head of the Olympic Village, Captain Wolfgang Furstner killed himself after being dismissed from the army. It had come to light that he had some Jewish heritage.

Helene Mayer returned to America after the Olympics. She never had a choice. She commented in a letter to friends in Germany: "It's all propaganda against Germany". She was not ready to give up on her homeland.

In 1937, she competed again against Ilona Schacherer-Elek and took the world championship. That year, German law removed all Jewish public servants, professionals, actors, musicians and journalists from their occupations. All Jewish-owned businesses were confiscated and all Jews were forced to take the same middle names; Israel for males and Sarah for all women.

Helene won the U.S. national championship again in 1938 and performed some public duty by teaching German to American soldiers as part of a special program at the University of California in Berkeley.

Helene's uncle Georg died in the Theresienstadt concentration camp in 1942. After the war, she was several times asked by friends if she regretted representing Nazi Germany at the Games and answered no. She told students at Mills College, however, that she had lost on purpose and been forced to compete. It seems that she had tremendous difficulty explaining to others, and perhaps to herself, how she had been so loyal to a nation that saw her as less than a person. The desire for acceptance, the emotional need to attach to the majority, even an oppressive majority, can be powerful.

Schmeling vs. Louis

In June 1936 Schmeling fought Joe Louis in New York. The Trollmann family and the world listened by radio.

Born the son of an Alabama sharecropper and raised from the age of twelve in Detroit, Joe Louis Barrow was destined to become only the second Black man to hold the heavyweight title. He loved sports growing up and once said he would have focused on baseball if there had been more opportunities for Blacks. Boxing was where the chance to rise was most available.

If the sport had a very Jewish fan base in the US, it also had the most racially integrated audience of any sport, though Blacks usually sat in cheaper seats and so the arena could be quite divided. Inter-racial fights were still rare enough to have a name; "mixed bouts". Jack Dempsey and many other top-ranked boxers, as noted previously, had refused to even take on Black opponents.

Schmeling had no hesitation about inter-racial competition.

Jacobs selected a training facility for Schmeling in the Catskills. It was inconveniently far from New York City but Jewish-owned. Norman Mailer has written that a training camp is "designed to manufacture one product – a fighter's ego." Jacobs saw a second and even higher criterion in choosing a site for training - the public image value. Louis also trained in a Jewish-owned facility whose owner, Harry Cohen arranged free board at a nearby mansion. The mansion's owner, also Jewish, was "not only a great admirer of the Brown Bomber, but wants to see Joe give Schmeling, the Nazi man a good trouncing."

The German press consistently portrayed Schmeling as an Aryan champion. It hardly mattered that the German Sports Ministry had come out against professional sports, stating often that every good athlete's goal should be national honor in amateur competition. The government did its best to promote Schmeling as the German who would beat inferior, foreign fighters. Goebbels' newssheet, the *Angriff* promoted special deals on cruise ships for Germans to go to New York to see the battle.

As in the past, the media pushed Schmeling to comment on the racial meaning of the fight. One reporter asked if, in Schmeling's experience, Blacks had less courage that whites. "In sport, the Negro and white man are just the same," he said. "The best man wins."

On the night before the fight, Black America found an unprecedented number of Americans rooting for a Negro hero. In general, Americans expected Louis to win; bookies put the odds at ten to one in his favor.[39] Ed Harris wrote in the Philadelphia Tribune: "Anything can happen now…Brothers, the battle is over…Soon you will be able to travel all over the Southland, marry women of other colors if you so desire, go anyplace and do anything."

In Germany the radio reminded everyone to tune in. "It is every German's obligation to stay up tonight. Max will fight overseas with a Negro for the hegemony of the white race!"

Top boxers Dempsey, Tunney, Baer and Braddock all spoke in favor of Louis. Dempsey said he would beat Schmeling in less than five rounds. Jesse Owens was known to be a fan. Nat Fleischer wrote in *Ring* magazine, "Louis is an American, and a darn good one at that." Fleischer, a New York Jew may have been a progressive but echoed views held around the country.

Even the positive media coverage of Louis was not free of racial commentary. The New York Sun wrote of him: "The American Negro is a natural athlete…generations of toil…have not obliterated the strength and grace of the African native."

The arena was filled on the big night. At ringside, viewers included J. Edgar Hoover, Bernard Baruch, Irving Berlin, George Burns, Joseph Pulitzer II, and Nelson Rockefeller.

Some Jewish organizations pushed for a boycott, not wishing to see Schmeling earn from ticket sales. Whatever his politics, he was a taxpayer in Nazi Germany and his wealth was his government's. Overall, the Jewish community did not rally behind the boycott effort. Three of the biggest Yiddish language newspapers, including the *Forverts* asked for press passes.

Weigh-in was at the Hippodrome, a Victorian hall on the corner of Sixth and 43rd Street. The fighters took photos, shook hands with the big shots in the business and went to the arena.

The fight at last began. Louis came out confident, throwing jabs. Schmeling's left eye quickly became puffy. Yet when they first clinched, Louis was said by commentators to be "filling in", throwing a lot of meaningless shots. It was a sign of a jittery fighter.

By the third round Schmeling was so bloody that one boxing commissioner shouted to stop the fight. The German was not so worried. "I think I knock him out," he told his corner men. "I have him where I want him." Schmeling put a right hand over high and brought it down on Louis's jaw. It shook his head. Louis, who had never fallen to the mat in his professional career, collapsed. He was only down for two seconds but it was a first.

By the tenth round, Louis was fumbling with his mouthpiece and the starting bell was delayed. Both men struggled on until the twelfth round.

Again, Louis was knocked down. He stayed there with one hand on the rope for four seconds, with the crowd expecting him to pull himself up. And then he landed face down on the canvas. The ringside announcer shouted: "Louis is down! Louis is down! Hanging to the ropes, hanging badly! He's a very tired fighter, he is blinking his eyes, shaking his head. The count is…the fight is over!"

The press missed no chance to add racial insult to physical injury. Bill Cunningham of the *Boston Post* wrote that the defeated Louis looked like a "grotesque Stepin' Fetchit type of a tired Negro".

Goebbels cabled "heartfelt congratulations" to Schmeling: "Our victory is a German victory."

Schmeling later remarked that it was not the way of an experienced boxer to hurry to his feet after a fall. One should stay calm and take time to clear his head.

Much can happen in a short time in boxing. Two years later, Schmeling had lost his title and Louis held it, making him the first Black heavyweight champion since Jack Johnson. Schmeling and Louis were set once again to enter the ring. The world heavyweight champion and a former champion had all the world's attention.

Schmeling returned to New York on a German cruise ship, the *Bremen*. When he came off the boat, all ten New York papers had a boxing reporter present. Wire services had sent their own people.

The fight was to be held at Yankee Stadium, where 70,00 fans had tickets to see it live. One hundred million worldwide listened on the radio, the largest audience that had ever tuned in for any event. At least twenty million Germans listened and, by some accounts, millions more. Sixty million tuned into the fight in America. It was three a.m. in Germany when the fight began. One German newspaper called it the "Night of the Bright Windows". It was five months before Kristallnacht, the Night of Broken Glass. Hitler cabled Schmeling: "To the next world's champion, Max Schmeling, Wishing you every success."

Harlem's hostels were full. People slept in cars. Louis predicted to the public that he would win in two rounds.

The venue was surrounded, and not only by ticket holders. Having failed to convince people to boycott the event, the Anti-Nazi League had volunteers on the street to give out flyers urging a boycott of German products. Communists too were giving out anti-Nazi pamphlets: "Schmeling Stands for Nazism"

Seats filled, as they had two years prior, with some of New York's and African American elite. A German paper commented on the "rich Harlem Negroes and their gem-laden wives". Cab Calloway, Louis Armstrong, Duke Ellington and countless others wore their best for the public and waited to see the Brown Bomber beat down widely-held theories.

Around the world people listened. Along with Rukeli, those tuned in included sixteen-year-old Angelo Dundee, who would become one of boxing history's best known trainers. He listened at his local fire station. In Lafayette, Alabama Louis' cousins listened at a Black restaurant. A jury in Trinidad listened on a radio in the middle of a murder trial. Schmeling's wife, Anny Ondra hid herself at home as the Nazi leadership and the public gathered in theaters and events around the country.

The fighters took photos, weighed in and went to dress. The boxing commission had forbidden Louis's favored brand of gloves because of the freedom of the thumb. It was a win for Jacobs. Someone commented that he had treated the issue as of the highest importance and seen the gloves as "not only a menace to his fighter, but also a violation of the Constitution, a reversal of the Dred Scott decision, an insult to the American flag, and an abuse of the Pure Food and Drugs Act". In the days before Don King, Jacobs was a character.

The audience cheered for the opening fighters but, as is usually the case, saved most of their enthusiasm for the main event.

When the title fight began, Ernest Hemingway wrote, Louis seemed "nervous and jumpy as a doped race horse". He was not the only witness to suggest that Louis might have been drugged for the occasion.

Barely twenty seconds in, Louis had Schmeling on the ropes. The crowd roared. The announcer could not talk fast enough to keep up with everything connecting to the German's head and body. Schmeling got in a blow to the jaw as Louis was stepping back from a clinch. German fans cheered but it was no victory. Louis had been moving away from it.

Louis stayed on top of him. He hit Schmeling with so many hard shots that the German let out a groan, or maybe it was cry, that was heard in the entire arena.

"I thought…how's that, Mr. Super-race?" Louis said later. "I was glad he was hurt."

Schmeling, after absorbing a body blow, stood in one place as he was hit in the face five times. Louis ended the flurry with two rights. Schmeling bent his knees and wobbled, hovering over the canvass. He held the ropes and did not exactly fall but was not exactly standing. He stayed there for an estimated half minute while the world waited. Richard Wright wrote that he "looked like a soft piece of molasses candy left out in the sun…he drooped over the ropes…powerful right arm hanging ironically useless." He went to one knee, then pulled himself back up a bit. The referee waved Louis away and began to count. Schmeling straightened up. Louis knocked him down and Schmeling again got up.

Louis pressed on. He knocked Schmeling down.

Again Schmeling stood but it was only for a moment. The same Schmeling who had commented two years earlier on Louis getting back into the fight too quickly now failed to take any time to breathe.

Another combination dropped him. He was drooling blood. Louis's last right to the face, according to the *Herald Tribune*, smashed him "like a baseball bat would an apple". The towel was thrown into the ring. Officially, this classic symbol of surrender was not a part of the rules in New York. The referee picked up the towel and threw it away, toward the ropes. Schmeling was now on his hands and knees.

His coach jumped into the ring. That did change things. The referee counted to five and then declared the fight over. "The count is five!" shouted the announcer. The referee counted on. The fight was declared a Technical Knock Out.

Schmeling had been defeated in one round.

There is a legend that German radio cut out when he was knocked down. Not so. The German radio announcer continued to praise

"Max" for his courage and determination. "Our Max, the Jews have poisoned him!" a German in the arena cried out.

In Harlem, people poured into the streets. A car pulled a banner; "BLACK RACE IS SUPREME TONIGHT". Traffic was stopped by a spontaneous festival on Seventh Avenue, between 116th and 145th Streets. In Washington, D.C., crowds flooded U Street. Celebrations went on across the country.

A few months later, in November the Nazis organized Kristallnacht. People smashed up Jewish shops and businesses and burned down Jewish houses of worship across Germany, Austria and the Sudetenland. David Lewin, an old friend of Schmeling's reached his door and asked for help hiding his two boys. Schmeling hid them in his apartment at the Excelsior Hotel in Berlin, telling the hotel that he was sick and should receive no visitors. When the pogroms died down, Schmeling helped the boys, Henry and Werner to sneak out of the country and reach the United States.

War Spreads

In 1938 the British ambassador to Berlin warned Germany's relatively new and emotional Foreign Minister, Joachim von Ribbentrop that amassing German troops on the border of Czechoslovakia might draw the world into war. Ribbentrop shouted at him. He was not known to keep cool. "Your British empire is an empty shell! It is rotten and decaying. It would have collapsed long ago were it not for Germany's support." He screamed at the British representative to butt out. The British ambassador stood, told the Minister off and went to the door. As he was leaving, Ribbentrop yelled after him. "Britain is governed by Jews, ha ha!" [40]

A few short months later, the Nazis took Czechoslovakia's Sudetenland and worked to build up the military with a mind to further conquests. Hitler's position and popularity increased. He had, after all, enlarged Germany without losing soldiers' lives. He had defied international opposition and called the world's powers' bluff.

Sinti and Roma in Hannover were forcibly removed from their homes and relocated to the *Altwarmbüchener Moor* (AM), a camp set up in moorlands in the Burgdorf area, where they would live in trailers. The new residents were kept living there for weeks before the city helped to dig a pit to provide drinking water. The Trollmanns were not among the people rounded up.

In March and April, the police arrested two thousand "work-shy" persons in the Reich to be brought to Buchenwald Concentration Camp; half of them were Sinti and Roma. Rukeli's brothers, who had work, stayed out of trouble for the moment.

Johann Trollmann was arrested and placed in the Hannover Ahlem Work Camp. He served several months there before going back to what had become normal life. When the war ended, Ahlem was liberated by the 84th Infantry Regiment of the U.S. Army. Information about the liberation came from a young military correspondent among the soldiers, a Jewish German immigrant to the United States named Henry Kissinger. This liberation, however, was still long years and millions of deaths away in 1938. Ahlem continued to menace those who could not find work or who attracted the attention of public servants.

In the summer, rationing began. Families were limited in their consumption of tea and coffee, bread, flour, cheese, sugar and other foods as well as soap, shoes and coal.

International call service stopped in September 1939. No explanation was given to the public. Operators told callers that normal service would resume shortly. It did not. The public's access to outside information was thereafter to be limited.

Germany had invaded Poland and Britain, as the ambassador had warned, was committed by treaty to come to the Poles' defense. Across the United Kingdom, people sat by wireless radios to hear their Prime Minister's somber words. Germany had made no reply to the British demand to draw back "Consequently, this country is at war with Germany."

A new rule was issued by Reinhard Heydrich, Deputy to the Chief of Police on the 1st of March, 1939. Sinti and Roma were to be documented and finally removed from the German "*Volkstum*", a term which Nazism took to mean the German race as well as culture. All Gypsies were to carry special identity cards that labeled them as pure Gypsies (brown ID), mixed Gypsies (blue striped ID cards) or people who were not Sinti or Roma but lived in a "Gypsy manner". (Such itinerants were given grey cards.) Here we see one of many odd inconsistencies in Nazi policy; while the system regarded Roma and Sinti as ethnic-biological groups and while the policies treated those who were completely assimilated into German society as just as dangerous as those who fit certain stereotypes, the Nazis also rounded up people with no Romani or Sinti blood who happened to be in a situation that the majority saw as *Gypsy-like*. The definition was racial but open enough that a white person without address or employment might end up with a grey card and punished as a Gypsy.

By 1943, authorities would list 21,498 people in Germany as Gypsies (not counting the grey cards), even after many had been removed from an original community of less than 15,000. A year later, the number would again grow to more than 23,900 mixed-race Gypsies despite the removal of so many. Some of this counter-intuitive population growth may be due to Roma escaping upheaval further east in Europe and entering Germany, hoping to make their way westward to freedom. Most of the growth, however, was the result of an ongoing government effort to trace family trees. Gypsies were found everywhere. Hitler's personal driver, Kurt Winterstein was removed from service (and sterilized) after his mother's Romani background was discovered. Even as Sinti and Roma were being taking off to concentration camps, more people were being identified as part Gypsy. At one point, the authorities would conclude that 80% of Gypsies in Germany were mixed.[41] For those who defined and counted Gypsies, the growth of a population marked for removal was not a problem; the government needed forced labor for armaments factories and a growing mixed race Gypsy roster only meant more slave labor.

It is often difficult for the modern historian to come up with precise numbers for the Sinti and Roma who died during the Holocaust. This is in part because so many people were executed by soldiers in forests and fields, or wherever they were found rather than arrested and brought to a center where records were carefully kept. It is also because many were sent to camps or killed ostensibly for other reasons. For example, the Sinto who Repplinger calls by the alias Hermann Schmidt was detained in 1938, not on racial grounds but because he was found to suffer from "congenital idiocy". He was to be sterilized. When his father filed an appeal, he was moved to the Observation-Station for the Mentally Ill in the Capital Hannover. A doctor there tested him and produced a report verifying his mental disability. He had failed to correctly answer such politically subjective queries as "What has the Fuhrer created?"

Not everyone in Europe was fully aware of what was happening inside the Reich. Django Reinhardt, Belgian-born and of French citizenship, traveled from France into Germany, crossing at Aachen while on his way to Denmark. He and the other members of his five-man band gave no thought to politics until they were pulled off their train and brought to a customs office for questioning. They were allowed, after all their money was taken, to continue on their way.

They looked out the train at the swastikas and at the throngs of soldiers at each station, unaware not only of how Germany was planning to take France but of what would then happen to Reinhardt and other members of his community.

Rukeli's brother Ferdinand Lolo Trollmann, like many Sinti, was taken to the *Polizeipräsidium* on Hardenberg Street to be examined. "I had to enter a room, in which many men, Gestapo…stood. One man, who I believe to have been Robert Ritter, the director of the Race-Hygienic Research Center in Berlin, greeted me in our language, Romanes."

Lolo was asked if he was a pure race Gypsy or mixed: "I answered him that I was a pure raced Gypsy," he wrote later. In response the man told him, "Then you have once again been lucky."

In a report to the German Research Society, Ritter remarked that "because a wide ranging evacuation is planned" he believed racial and biological research on Gypsies had to be conducted urgently. After all, he wrote, "the people who [are] currently available shortly will be taken away from scientific experimentation…"

On trial after the war, Ritter argued that he did not know what the government would do with his research or that there was a plan to put Gypsies into concentration camps, let alone to make sure that they never walked back out. The quotation above shows a considerably less naïve view.

Returning to October 1939, authorities in Hannover received a detention decree from the Reich Criminal Police for the immediate arrest of all Gypsies. Two days later, orders were handed down within the police force for treatment of full-blooded and mixed Gypsies. They were to be confined to their homes. If they left, they were to be arrested and transferred to a concentration camp. This was the beginning of the enactment of Heinrich Himmler's plan to remove all Gypsies from "Greater Germany" to occupied Poland. Himmler was, at this point in his career, head of the SS as well as a leader in the party and in the set-up and management of the concentration and extermination camps.

Django Reinhardt, in neighboring France, remained unaware of the conditions his brethren faced just a border away. Django was performing jazz at a new cabaret in Paris, the Hot Feet. One night, Duke Ellington and his bass player came in at around two in the morning, having heard of the young performer. They had a drink with Django and then Ellington sat at the bar's piano and they improvised, playing together. Ellington and the members of his band knew no French and Django's English was limited to some jazz lingo like "yeah, man" but they managed to communicate and discussed the possibility of touring together in America. One should not misunderstand here that life for all the Gypsies in France was just business as usual. Django's good fortune was as unusual as his talent.

In Germany, on the 27th of April 1940, 2,500 Gypsies were sent to Poland on the basis of a letter from Himmler known as the "G-Resettlement Decree". Three hundred were sent to ghettos in Poland or to the Auschwitz-Birkenau concentration camp. When the first Roma and Sinti arrived in the camp, their containment area was not even ready to receive them. Administrative buildings were still under construction. The Roma and Sinti prisoners were put in wooden barracks that had been originally meant as stalls for horses. They were thirty-two windowless shelters with slits in the roof for ventilation. From 1940, entire families detained at Altwarmbüchener Moor were sent on the camps, in particular Auschwitz. The "Gypsy Central Office" controlled these movements. Its staff decided which Sinti would be deported to the camps, which would be sterilized, and which should do forced labor. Later, the Roma and Sinti deported to Poland were declared "enemies of the Reich", allowing for their real estate and other assets to be expropriated by the government and sold off. In Berlin and other cities, authorities used the same forms for property confiscation that were used for Jews, just crossing out the word Jew and writing Gypsy in its place. In many cases, by force of habit, the bureaucrat even assigned the Sinti and Romani women the middle name Sarah, as was done with Jews.

It is estimated that anywhere between a third and half of Germans knew that the victims being deported to the east were to be mass murdered.[42] How aware were Sinti and Roma of what was ahead?

Not all had heard the same information and not all believed. Some received no stories of the camps, yet many were in the military. As will be discussed later, tales of what happened in the camps did come home, even if some chose not to believe the horror stories.

The Trollmanns were living in a very different Hannover than the city of Rukeli's childhood. Since 1937, the government had been systematically razing the Old Town. Urban planners aimed to redesign the poorest neighborhoods for "eradication of the morally sub-standard and the biologically defective". White-collar workers and city employees filled the new constructions while the poor residents moved to public housing in Ricklingen and Mecklenheide.

Sinti and Roma were banned from Nazi organizations. Family friend Edu Weiss had long remained a member of the *Jungvolk*, a section of the Hitler Youth. "We stood in our uniforms in the street whenever Jews were collected and yelled 'Jews out' and 'You're getting what you deserve.'... I had no idea what was really wrong." He was surprised when the Fuhrer of his youth group informed him that he was being dismissed as a non-Aryan. In the year the Nazis took control of the Reichstag, Hitler Youth group memberships had grown from 50,000 to more than two million. In 1936, membership for minors became compulsory and the ranks of members more than doubled. Being cast out was unthinkable for Edu. *Everyone* was a member.

As the efforts to cleanse the German home territory of alien elements went on, the war wit external forces put its own demands on resources, and especially human resources. Jews had been forbidden from military service. Gypsies, while no longer German for years, were not yet specifically excluded from military service. As the government called up men for service, many Sinti were summoned and went. Lolo Trollmann reported in 1942 for service in the *Luftwaffe*, or Air Force and would rise to the rank of corporal.

In November 1939, Rukeli received a letter conscripting him into the infantry. He served first in Schlesien, then went out of the country to Poland, then Belgium, on to the Somme, the Loire, Normandy, and back again to Poland. While Sinti and Roma were going to the concentration camps of Poland to die, others were fighting for the regime committing the genocide. This is not only true of Germany.

How can one make sense of Sinti and Roma serving in the German and other fascist countries' militaries at such a time? Most were drafted and given no choice. Many were also patriots. Some were following in the footsteps of fathers and grandfathers who had also served their countries in war. Romani American Holocaust education activist Bill Duna worries about a book that exposes Roma and Sinti as soldiers on the side of evil. It is not how we would like to remember our people. "How do we show that it's not like they wanted to fight? Because we've had enough of people thinking we're all unethical Gypsies... A lot of people had no choice but to follow along with their government." True enough, and perhaps even more true for the weakest members of society than for Aryans. And yet we cannot presume that soldiers like Rukeli had no desire to prove that they were full members of German society and, despite common prejudices, as courageous and connected to their *patria* as anyone else.

Across the divide, Roma were also struggling on the other side of the war. In May 1940 German Luftwaffe planes dropped bombs on along the Belgian-French border. A group of Roma watched in terror from the woods.[43] They were of the Lowara tribe, known to other Roma for their skill in horse breeding. This particular "camp" or *kumpania* of families divided their time between Francophone Europe, Serbia and points in between. Their semicircle of over a dozen wagons shook with commotion, people hurriedly jumping from bedcovers and eiderdowns to see what was happening. Women screamed, ripped their clothes and rolled their heads from side to side as they did at funerals and wakes.

As they gathered their horses and prepared to move, the bomber planes disappeared into the distance. When the Roma went onto the main road going south, they found it already packed with refugees. Trucks, cars, buses, bikes, pushcarts and many people on foot clogged the way. Churches, schools and public buildings were turned to shelters. At times, the German planes returned and indiscriminately strafed the fleeing civilians. After a couple days on the roads, the masses were disheveled, filthy, unshaven and dazed.

The wagon-bound Roma stood out in that they were largely at home. Non-Roma had lost their businesses, their possessions and their way. The Lowara were used to having only what their wagons carried. For them, at least at first, the refugee path meant less change than it did for others. They were already trained survivalists who knew how to pick campsites near the roads with flowing water and some shade. Their wagons were built to go off road when necessary and they had experience raiding for a goose or chicken when all else failed.

With an elder named Pulika leading the group's decisions of which way to go, they crossed into France, hoping to find safety from the war. The advancing German army, however, did not stop in Belgium and the violence could not be outrun. They were at the River Somme, where Rukeli fought for the German aggressors.

Soon Paris was taken and an armistice was signed. Speaking to other refugees at the Somme, the Lowara learned that the French police were arresting Loyalist Spaniards who had gone into France to escape fascism in their own country. Under the same security measures, thousands of Gypsies also were being rounded up for proven or assumed anti-fascist views and interned in camps such as Le Vernet, Mulhouse and Sarthe. In the southwest of the country, several hundred Gypsies were imprisoned in the Saliers concentration camp, in a village of the same name within the municipal limits of Arles. Among the camp's residents was Jose Reyes, whose sons would one day found the *Gipsy Kings* music group.

Gypsies in the newly occupied lands also began to be used for slave labor in state-owned factories. More were turned over, from the French authorities to the Gestapo and "processed" to the east.

Pulika's Lowara were not as naïve as some Roma or Sinti. They had sensed the growing danger before the German army came west. They had attempted to immigrate to the New World. Illiterate and living day to day, they were not nearly as capable of making visa applications and making their way onto ships for New York as they were of bribing and sneaking their way across Europe's land borders. Now it was too late to escape. They were inside fascist Europe.

It was not, however, too late to fight back. Among the tribe was a white boy fluent in Romani, French and other languages. Jan Yoors, a Flemish teen had been informally adopted by the tribe's patriarch when he was just twelve and spent his youth back and forth between the Roma and his biological family. Yoors broke off from the Roma and went to Paris, thinking that he would stay briefly at a convent on the Boulevard Arago, run by a Mother Superior who was close to his parents and then go on to London, where he could enlist in the war effort. He found that there was no need to go to London. One night at the convent, he was visited by a man of unknown origin who made Yoors an offer to serve in a different way. He wanted Yoors to liaise between the Roma and the anti-German underground. He was no more specific than that about whom he represented. Yoors agreed and returned to the Roma with a new French name and papers. The Roma too, when he told them what had happened, agreed to join the movement.

Life grew hard under occupation. Nomadic Roma did not dare to light campfires at night. Yoors noticed that mosquitos fed upon the Roma in the evening like never before with no smoke to chase them away. Social ties were cut, with tribes split up to travel in smaller, more discreet groups. The Lowara worked to alter the appearances of their horses, to make them look sickly and less worth the German's taking. Nonetheless, they were stopped on the road by soldiers and many of their horses were confiscated. Roma were not the only victims of the Germans' horse "requisitions". Roma and white farmers gathered to discuss horse trading at certain pubs and shared stories of how they often ran into the woods and to hide with their horses, on rumors that the Germans were coming.[44]

The loss of one's animals was not the worst risk for members of an inferior race. Many of the Roma changed their clothing and, when interacting with outsiders, would claim to be of other ethnicities; they told people they were Armenians or Christian Arabs. Others passed as Latin American merchants in order to avoid arrest.

At a roadside inn, the leader of the tribe, Pulika met the inn's owner, who asked him quietly about smuggling contraband. When Pulika expressed interest and made small talk, the innkeeper slowly let out that the cargo would be a friend who needed to escape. Pulika agreed to sneak the man out "as a friend", with no fee. The deal was sealed with a brandy toast. That night the human cargo was brought to the Roma's camp, given a last drink of water and helped into a storage bin in the underside of a wagon, where the Roma normally carried spare chains, harness and equipment.

Hours later, a tobacco farmer was arrested and taken away by the Gestapo. The passenger was still hiding in the storage bin days later when a group of *gendarmes,* or national police stopped the Roma for a routine document check. One of the gendarmes approached Pulika's wagon and kicked lightly at the storage crate. It was the first time a policeman had ever looked there. The Roma said that there was no key and offered to go into town to borrow a hacksaw. The gendarme let the matter go. Had he been working with information from an interrogation and given up so easily? Or had he been trying to warn the Roma? In any case, it was a close call.

The incident did nothing to discourage more of the same risk taking. The tribe went on to smuggle more people and soon began to help the resistance by carrying explosives and small weapons. As Yoors recalls, "We were aware of being part of a spreading pattern of resistance that was to grow into an invisible but solid wall of systematic opposition."

Yoors's handler in Paris ordered him to recruit a cadre of young Roma open to greater participation, who would receive specialized training. What kind of training was not explained.

The man recognized, he said, that the Roma would want more of a sign than Yoors's word that the resistance wanted and respected the cooperation of the Roma. Pulika would discuss involvement with the Resistance at an upcoming *kris,* or Romani court, a large meeting of elders. The man asked the kris to choose a coded phrase that they wanted to hear on the BBC. On an agreed day, the code words would be delivered in a broadcast from London for all the Roma to hear as a verbal contract. If the Roma would help the resistance, "they" would offer a general amnesty after the war.

An amnesty for what exactly? What crimes had they committed and what slate would be wiped clean? It did not matter. The Roma neither trusted nor expected a long-term promise from outsiders. If they risked their lives, it was not with any exchange of favors in mind.

The kris was held in an inn where the owner did not mind, at least in such a difficult economy, having a hoard of Gypsies for guests. The establishment had recently been refurbished in an international, modern style with tubular chrome around the bar ad green leather upholstery. Everything smelled, when the Roma arrived, of new linoleum and varnish. The owner tended to bottles behind a long bar as the Roma gathered. They kept their wide-brimmed hats on indoors, the size of their hats a status symbol. Pulika spoke to the gathering. They knew, he said, that the Germans had arrested many Roma who never were seen again. The Nazis' intentions were clear enough. As Yoors recalled later, Pulika advised the other elders "only fish allow themselves to be caught twice by the same hook".

Not everyone was convinced. Pani, an elder of the Tchurara tribe said that "*o shoshoy kaste si feri yek khiv sig athadjol.*" The rabbit that has only one hole is soon caught. And so, he said, it was time to run and hide or to be eaten. "Aren't we giving new names to old troubles?...It is better to be at least a moving target."[45]

Pulika reminded that rabbits in danger "are known to become insane [stupid] with fear. Until now the Germans are still fighting against other enemies everywhere and, partly as a matter of luck, we are left alive. If the Germans win their war, if they are left to devour the world, they will hunt us down."

Members of the Lowara, Tchurara and Kalderash tribes were asked to pledge to work against the Germans. All the Roma needed to be united, Pulika said. One of the other tribes' elders offered an oath. "May my curse and the curse of the kris…precede and follow to the grave him who falls short of the obligations of kinship. Cursed be he who, even inadvertently, helps our enemies."

Pulika explained that the high-ups of the resistance offered to help their Romani partners. They could share intelligence to warn of

German raids and could offer hiding places, some money, fake identity papers and even guns and explosives.

"Even crumbs are bread," someone said.

The kris went on for hours and ended without an agreement of all. Some joined and others made no commitment. Pulika was satisfied. He had made his intentions for his kumpania known and nobody had gone against him. If not all planned to take part, he had consent and could do as he chose.

The gathered were woken in the morning by submachine gun fire and German shouting. For a moment, it seemed that they had been caught before they ever really started. Going outside, the Roma learned that the cause of the excitement was only some kites. The trigger-ready Germans opened fire at flying objects before recognizing them for harmless toys.

Yala and Paprika, members of Pulika's tribe. Taken 1933-34, Jan Yoors

The Pot Boils

Rukeli went home on leave in the winter of 1940-41. There, he consoled young Edu Weiss on his ostracism from the Hitler Youth. He let the boy hold his gun. "It was too heavy," Edu later remembered. Rukeli bought him sweets and played soccer with him in the street. "He was a big kid," Edu said. "Playful and funny."

In Slovakia at this same moment, a fascist government that followed the German example also conscripted Roma even as discussions began for removing them from Slovakia to the death camps. One young soldier, when he first encountered Soviet troops on the battlefield, raised his rifle with his white t-shirt tied to the end as a flag and shouted, "Don't shoot! I'm Gypsy!" He defected and eventually returned home to Slovakia as part of the Soviet invasion. In Communist Czechoslovakia, his sons would become some of the very few Roma to attend university. All would become wealthy. One of the sons, Emil Scuka became a government prosecutor and in time, as the system began to crumble, a signatory along with playwright Vaclav Havel (a friend from days in university theater groups) of the anti-Communist movement's Charter 77. Emil Scuka became a leader of the anti-communist Velvet Revolution and the founder of the Romani political party, Romani Civic Initiative (ROI), winning a seat in Parliament in the country's first free, post-communist elections. The genocide and its survival stories cast shadows over those at the center of today's stories.

In May 1941, Rukeli went into Infantry Regiment 12. He fought as a rifleman, or *Schütze*. Like Scuka, he was deployed to fight the Soviet Union. Unlike the Slovak Romani soldier, Rukeli did not flee to the other side. He was wounded in Sobolew.

While Sinti like Trollmann fought for Germany against the USSR, Germany threw the last Roma and Sinti children out of its schools. In the autumn, Germany rounded up thousands of Sinti and other Gypsies in Austria and deported them to the Jewish ghetto of Lodz, in occupied Poland. The Gypsy camp, isolated even from the rest of the already sealed off (Jewish) ghetto, was the first site where Roma and Sinti were prepared for extermination in a camp setting. Roughly half would die in the first few months due to starvation and disease. 4,996 Roma and Sinti were sent to Lodz from Germany, Austria and other countries (who were first briefly held in transit in temporary camps in Austria). Those who did not die were sent on, with the Jews of the ghetto, to be exterminated by gas in 1942 in Chelmno.

While Gypsies bled on the front in the Nazis' army, tens of thousands of Soviet Sinti and Roma were exterminated en masse by the Einsatzgruppen and Sicherheitspolizei: men, women and children were slaughtered in mass shootings as their villages were burned. When Germany took control of Soviet territories, it did not develop one uniform policy for how to deal with the local Roma but left decisions about whom to round up and execute to local agencies. In some areas, the directives were to round up the nomadic Roma. In practice, sedentary Roma were just as likely to be arrested. Research has shown that "no sedentary Roma ever apprehended by the German military authorities… avoided a firing squad."[46]

One officer reported: "The shooting of Jews is simpler than that of the Gypsies. One has to admit that the Jews go to their death composed – they stand whereas the Gypsies cry, scream and move…Several even jump into the ditch and pretend to be dead."

In Latvia, the Baltic state with the highest pre-war Romani population and where many Roma were landowners, it is estimated that more than half the community died. The Germans worked closely with local sympathizers, the Latvian Auxiliary Police, who killed many Roma themselves. In the rest of the Soviet Union, the percentage is the same. The German invasion halved the Soviet Romani population.[47]

The contradiction of Roma and Sinti doing compulsory military duty within an organization dedicated to the extermination of their people continued until February 1941, when a military internal memorandum reported: "Gypsies and persons with noticeable elements of Gypsy blood (mixed-Gypsies) are not suitable to active duty." Even then, some caveats were offered: "This determination is not to be applied all over, especially for those who have excellent service or are suggested for an award."

Some Roma and Sinti did serve even after February 1941. Rukeli was eligible for special consideration and might still have received an award for his combat duty. However, the Gypsy Central Office questioned his suitability during a home leave visit. He had rubbed someone the wrong way and every civil servant of any rank had the power of life and death over the Sinti.

In the summer of 1941 Gypsies were moved en masse to forced labor and extermination camps.

After Germany began its attack of the U.S.S.R. in June, resistance groups in Nazi-occupied Europe became even more fractured than previously. It is not surprising that the small resistance community within Germany had little interest in forming cooperation with Roma (or Jewish) underground; much of the German anti-Nazi thought leadership was grounded in Christian, conservative and racist ideals. While against Nazism because of pro-peace beliefs, the ideology of much of Germany's anti-Nazi leadership was just as rooted in the notion of the superiority of the German *volk* as the Nazis' own.[48] Outside Germany the resistance effort, which had been complicated enough, was now ever more confused by local groups' divergent political agendas. Groups were left or right-leaning, some had pro-Soviet and others had strong anti-communist alignments. Many underground organizations in the occupied lands coped by having a very limited focus, avoiding conflict with other partisans. Some exclusively worked on hiding political refugees or rescuing Jewish children. Others helped to bring Allied pilots who were shot down in German-held territory to safe houses and then transferred them away via complex routes. Still, politics confounded resistance. Historian Robert Gildea believes it is more correct to "talk less about the French Resistance than about resistance in France"[49], as the effort was neither unified nor carried out exclusively by ethnic and native French. Cooperating with the Roma was not to every group's taste and pre-war prejudices did not disappear in all quarters.

For Roma staying at partisan hideouts in the woods of France, interethnic misunderstandings brought tension. One point of stress was food. Partisans ate whatever they could and did not understand why Roma, even at risk of starvation, refused to break their dietary laws. Horsemeat was an acceptable meal to the Frenchmen but not to the Roma. Worse, the French partisans were units of men with no women while the Roma left behind with them were usually women whose men were off attending to other matters. When the French men asked the Romani women to take in their washing, the women refused. To the French, this seemed pointlessly rude. To the Romani women, handling outside men's clothing, especially pants or underclothes, was a taboo.

Yoors and some of the young Roma he recruited, meanwhile, were trained in demolitions. Young members of the Lowara and Tchurara tribes took high-risk orders from a central command about which they knew little. They trusted in shared goals and asked nothing more.

They were correct to sense urgency in their mission. With the Wannsee Conference of January 20th, 1942, the intended genocide or *Völkermord* of the Jews was put into place. No special conference was needed for Sinti and Roma. They were included in the mass execution without any special mention. It was an afterthought. In July 1942, an order from the High Command of the Wehrmacht removed all Gypsies from active service for "racial-political reasons". Rukeli and Lolo were both released from service. That same year, Justice Minister Thierack wrote after a meeting with Goebbels: "Regarding the extermination of the asocial lives, Dr. Goebbels stands by the position that the Jews and the Gypsies… should be exterminated."

Raids on public housing continued in Hannover, with police rounding up those Roma and Sinti who were still free. The Weiss family was arrested in October. As they and other Sinti were loaded into military trucks, a father asked where their new apartment was. Soldiers had they were relocating to a new apartment. One of the guards pointed to a livestock wagon. That, he told him, was the place for Gypsies.

Many of Rukeli's family went to Liebenau, to a Labor-Education Camp or *Arbeitserziehungslager*. There were wooden barracks in the woods, surrounded by barbed wire. Along with German Gypsies, the camp held Polish, Russian and Belarussian forced laborers who would fill their time in service to the Eibia-Wolff & Co. armament company.

Among the prisoners were Rukeli's old Sinti neighbor Berta Bluma Weiss and her brother Goldi, Robert Weiss and Rukeli's brothers Julius, Mauso and Benny. Werner Carlo Fahrenholz remembers: "The work was hellishly difficult. For any problem, they got 25 lashes with a horsewhip. The prisoners wore Wehrmacht jackets with an 'H' on the back. In the morning was a thin piece of bread, a dollop of margarine, a dollop of marmalade, and a cup of coffee substitute." *Muckefuck* is the German word he used for the coffee. "Roll call was at 6 AM and then the SS let them stand for an hour. To work at 7…I was 16 years old and terribly afraid." [50]

The SS executed prisoners often. And they were not the only masters. Kapos, convicts given supervisory roles in camps, "were bad, worse than the SS."[51]

Hitler's favorite filmmaker, Leni Riefenstahl was working on her latest project, a feature film called *Lowlands*. Over budget and behind schedule (she had begun filming in 1940), Riefenstahl had given herself the starring role as Marta, a mysterious dancer and wanderer who drifts into the village of Rocabruna, run by a wicked marquis who denies the peasants access to water. Marta quickly has the marquis and all the townspeople fascinated with her wild, unbridled beauty. Riefenstahl wanted dark extras to play the peasants of her village. She wanted Gypsies. She arranged for captive Sinti and Roma in the concentration camp at Maxglan, near Salzburg in Austria to be brought temporarily from the camp to work for her. The film director personally examined the camp inmates and chose her talent. She had others brought in from the Berlin-Marzahn camp. As they were forbidden to travel on public transit, she used her high level contacts with the government to make special arrangements to get them to the filming location.

"The Gypsies, both adults and children, were our darlings," she said years after. "We saw nearly all of them after the war." This claim is impossible, as most of them died when she was done with them. She recalled that the Sinti and Roma called her Aunt Leni and that they told her "the work with us was the most beautiful time of their lives." It was also very close to the end of their lives. After having them play her imaginary village's maids and servants, dress in Mediterranean costumes and applaud her dancing, she was finished with them. She made no calls and wrote no letters to seek to keep them from the concentration camps. A checked list of sixty-five of her Sinti and Roma extras turned up at least twenty-nine who died in Auschwitz-Birkenau.[52] How many of them died in other camps has not been studied.

At the end of the year came Himmler's Auschwitz Decree, sent to all Criminal Police Centers in the Reich with the heading "Regarding: Admission of mixed-Gypsies, Rom-Gypsies, and Balkan Gypsies into a Concentration Camp". All Gypsies in Greater Germany, regardless of whether they were mixed or pure and regardless of their housing or employment, were to be moved toward Auschwitz's Gypsy Camp IIe. This ended a long-running debate between Himmler and others in the party leadership regarding the possibility of a small reservation, inspired by American Indian reservations. Himmler had advocated for some time that a small community of pure blood Gypsies should be allowed to survive and to have a territory, perhaps in Poland, where they could live in peace. The plan was now put to rest. There were to be no Roma and Sinti in the future Reich-governed Europe.

Auschwitz-Birkenau became the largest extermination center of all for Roma and Sinti. Former guards recall Sinti arriving in military uniform and displaying their combat service medals. One was an officer who had received the Iron Cross and did the Nazi salute on arrival. Even a senior party member, whose grandfather had been a Gypsy from Leipzig, found himself deported to Auschwitz.

By mid-1943, most German Sinti and Roma had been sent to the camps and would make up almost two-thirds of Auschwitz-Birkenau Gypsy Camp, followed by Roma and Sinti from the Protectorate of Bohemia and Moravia (today's Czech Republic). On arrival, they were tattooed with a number and the prefix Z, for *Zigeuner* or Gypsy. In March, removal of the Gypsies held in Altwarmbüchener Moor began. A train went from there, from one town to next, west to east, stopping to collect people on the way to Auschwitz.

Dr. Josef Mengele was one of the personalities waiting for them at Auschwitz who would become infamous and who enjoyed contact with Sinti and Roma. One survivor of his experiments, Rita Prigmore is best known for a single photo. Her face is haunting and recognizable to many Roma and Sinti. There is no more often used photo to accompany the story of Roma and Sinti in the Holocaust than the black and white image taken in Mengele's research facilities in Auschwitz where the child Rita and her twin sister waited for his cruelty to begin. The sister perished. Rita has chronic pain until today as a result of the damage. She has written to everyone from the US Holocaust Memorial Museum to Oprah Winfrey in search of someone to help translate a German book about her family's fate. Her family, the Wintersteins are mentioned in the opening pages. They had been landowners for years and supplied grapes to wineries. The German administration confiscated their home and business. Most of the family died in Auschwitz. In 1987, Rita received compensation money from West Germany.[53]

Helmut Clemens, an assistant to Mengele, was an eyewitness to the doctor's work. "I was… with Mengele whenever he chose twins for his experiments, I had to bring them to him…During his experiments, I wasn't allowed to be there, he always sent me out. I was once, however, in the room with him by coincidence… I saw how the children received liquid in the eyes, then got gigantic eyes. Some days later, I saw the children dead in the corpse barracks. Dr. Mengele did experiments like this, and others, every second or third day in the camp." Mengele murdered twins with heart injections and sent their eyes for further scientific evaluation to the Kaiser-Wilhelm Institute for Anthropology in Berlin.

Mengele was simultaneously on contract to the director of the Berlin Kaiser-Wilhelm-Institute for Anthropology and, under this agreement, performed experiments on prisoners in regard to eye color and other genetic traits. Hundreds were tortured, crippled and killed under his projects. He brought much of his work to Barracks

32 of the Gypsy Family Camp for experiments on "the rabbits", as his SS doctors called the victims.

While the amusements of men like Mengele were a threat to the prisoners, they were not the only dangers. Noma and other diseases were prevalent in Auschwitz due to malnutrition. The Jewish doctor Lucie Adelsberger reported: "The kids' block of the Gypsy camp was not much different than the adults'. But it was much more painful to see the kids. Both kids and adults were skin and bones. No muscle, no fat."

The Jewish and Gypsy prisoners, though not living in the same barracks, had daily interaction at Auschwitz just as in other camps. The grandchild of one Dachau survivor retells interethnic incomprehension: "Jewish and other mothers would ask Romani women to kill their small children before they were gassed, beaten to death, or taken away...They thought that Romani women could perform hexes and curses and would help their children die peacefully. I guess they were pretty desperate."[54]

As some prisoners were moved to Auschwitz, others were moved into Altwarmbüchener Moor to wait for their turn. Rukeli's mother, Friederike and brother Lolo were there. Lolo remembered: "...train cars and wooden partitions were abandoned. Without sanitary facilities and without a water place, we had to get drinking water from the...ground and boil it". The arrests and relocation to the camp were led by Heinrich Harms from the Gypsy Central Office. He spoke Sinti well and knew the Trollmanns. He sometimes warned members of the Weiss and Fahrenholz families when to hide. Parents took their children to a tavern in Ricklingen to sit for a few hours before going home. He did not feel the same duty to help Rukeli's family.

Rukeli's older brother, Carlo stayed out of the camps a long time. He was married to an Aryan woman, Erna and they had six children. He was taken and interrogated often. His brother Ferdinand's wife, who was an office worker and understood bureaucracy, went and talked to the police to bring him back out onto the street. It also helped that Carlo was employed at a freight depot as a foreman, loading guns onto trains. He hoped this sort of position would help and it did. He hid members of the Weiss family in his home at times.

Gypsies received half the food rations of impoverished whites and feeding the children required finding a neighbor who would share food (without informing police of the presence of Gypsies). A neighbor named Mrs. Reuter frequently shared her rations. Carlo's daughter Inga hid in her place when police came around. Mrs. Reuter promised to take Inga in if the rest of the family were arrested. "My daughter Inga was the only of my children to have light hair and thus would not be immediately recognized as a Sintezza," wrote Erna.

In Paris, jazz was the craze and Django Reinhardt was its master. One photo preserved years after the war showed Django in front of the Cigale nightclub with German soldiers in uniform and with other jazz musicians, including a German officer, a Romani, several Black men and a Jew. The Nazi *Komandatur* in charge in Paris sent word to Django. He was requested to travel to Berlin with his *Nouveau Quintette* to perform live for the Nazi High Command. Glad to still be alive and free in Paris, Django was terrified at the idea of going into the belly of the beast. He stalled. He set a ridiculously high fee and hoped to enter lengthy negotiations. This was no use. The Komandatur's office informed him that going to Berlin was obligatory. Django, left untouched for so long, went into hiding. He traveled with his wife and mother to the Swiss border, hoping to escape to neutral territory. His fancy car, a Buick needed more gasoline than he had the ration cards to buy. He ran out of gas and ration cards at Annecy, not more than 30 miles from the border crossing. There, he sold off the car in a hurry and bought train tickets. Arriving at the town of Thonon near the border, he and the women stayed with other Manouche and made contact with a family of scrap metal dealers who crossed the border every day. He made a deal that they would smuggle the Reinhardts across for a price. And they failed. The border guards sent Django and his family back toward France with a warning.

Django turned back to Paris, where he feared both capture by the authorities and Allied bombing. At least he had money, celebrity and connections. He found a new villa around the corner from the place

Pigalle. It was both a short walk from the cabarets and a short walk to the Pigalle metro (subway) station. The station was one of the deepest and best shelters in the city.

The music that Django played, and that African American GI's had brought in since World War I was not only a hit in France. Jazz was hot in Germany despite and perhaps a bit because of governmental disdain. Swing kids, as the teens who embraced jazz were called, listened to it at private house parties and wherever they could find it. The boys backcombed their hair with brilliantine in rejection of the paradigmatic short, military style haircuts and girls grew the long, groomed hair they saw in Hollywood films whereas girls in the League of German Girls (Nazi youth groups) wore traditional braids. Swing girls wore the pinched-waist, slimming outfits that were popular in Paris and America or the trouser suits that Katherine Hepburn made cool, and that Hitler vocally loathed. The swing kids were not on the streets of Rukeli's old neighborhood. They were middle and upper class youth with money, even as so much was falling apart, for trendy fashion and for going to parties. In the Trollmanns' part of town, people wore what clothes had the fewest holes. Choices of music and clothes, like all choices, were increasingly limited.

As war raged on, bomb attacks on rail lines slowed the pace at which Germany could move its minorities to the camps in Poland. After an attack on the 9th of October, 1943, Edu Weiss remembers, the transport in Hannover completely stopped. There was also almost no one left to deport. Sinti were forbidden to enter bunkers and shelters during attacks. When Erna went to a clinic shortly before she gave birth to her son Wolfgang, she was denied entrance to the cellar of the hospital. "They told me, we don't take Gypsies anymore."

Police officers combed Hannover for Sinti who had remained hidden. The rationing of food and essential goods since 1939 had created an enormous black market. This underground economy and network of thieves who stole from government warehouses, gangsters who trafficked in the products and affiliated illicit business people, all the result of Nazi austerity, were an unintended haven for those who sought to evade the authorities. "Submarines" as Germans came to call the fugitives who hid from the Nazis, living under the radar, included an estimated five to seven thousand Jews at one point. Many made use of the crime networks for help in finding illegal and unregistered shelter and provisions. Many Sinti and Roma did the same.

Ten-year-old Sinto Fritz Laubinger watched an arrest on Hofgrefe Street: "My grandfather lived in Stöcken as a respected resident. He operated a horse and cart, with which he transported the mail of the city of Hannover and took over the transport for the supply depot of the army. On the early morning of the 18th of February 1944, a Gestapo truck drove up. We had to stand in front of the door in the yard. The Gestapo called the names of our relatives from a list... They were driven, some in their pajamas, onto the truck and brought to a collection camp in the Gestapo Central Office on Hardenberg Street. As the list was read through, the people cried... I have seen this with my own eyes, because I stood…in the yard. This action was led by a Commissar Harms, who spoke our language…and knew our nicknames."[55]

By this time boys as young as twelve were being rounded up and conscripted into service in the SS and military units in some parts of the country. In Berlin even children were handed bazookas and shown how to shoot them. The Soviets were coming, they said. If they took German cities, nobody knew what horrors they would do in return for their families' deaths at the hands of German invaders.[56]

In 1944 the Nazis planned to hasten the extermination of Gypsies. The Gypsy prisoner population of Auschwitz-Birkenau was to be put to an end in May. On May 16th, the SS intended to move the vast majority of Roma and Sinti from their barracks in Gypsy Camp B IIe to the gas chambers. Plans, however, were leaked shortly before the action was to begin. The camp commander, a German named Georg Bonigut had told one of his prisoner clerks, Tadeusz Joachimowski of the plan to gas all the Gypsies. He found a moment to go and warn some of them.

The prisoners acted quickly, hoping against the odds and identifying any possible weapon. Hand shovels, iron piping, hand-made knives and even rocks from the ground around the barracks were better than bare hands. Emaciated victims young and old readied themselves and, when the guards arrived, they barricaded themselves into their barracks. The camp administration assessed the risks and called off the massacre. All summer prisoners survived, knowing that their captors' aim was to kill them all and knowing that they would fight until the end. Through the early summer, most of the working age males were moved to other parts of Auschwitz for work detail and met their deaths away from their families.

On June 6, 1944 the Allies landed at Normandy Beach in France. The American forces were under the command of General Dwight Eisenhower, the son of a German-American father and a half Black mother. Manouche musician Armand Stenegry, later better known by the stage name Archange, led other Manouche partisans on raids to support the invasion. Paris spent the summer waiting for liberation. The Nazis were determined to stop the resistance and to kill any suspected underground members.

Django Reinhardt focused on his new club, the *Roulotte-Chez Django Reindhardt (the caravan – home of Django Reinhardt)* on rue Pigalle and cared for a newly born son, Babik.

At twilight on August 2, 1944 trucks with wooden siding arrived at the Gypsy Camp, by then home mostly to the elderly, women and children. Prisoners were given sausages and bread and told to get ready to be taken to a new camp. The first truckloads began their path, then turned. They were heading for the gas chambers and crematoria. People began to scream. The final liquidation phase of the camp had begun. "An SS guard told me how much more difficult this special action had been than anything else which had ever been carried out in Auschwitz… The Gypsies, who knew what was in store for them, screamed. Fights broke out, shots went off and people were wounded. SS reinforcements arrived when the trucks were only half full. The Gypsies even tried to use hard loaves of bread as missiles. But the SS were too strong…too numerous," recalls Dazlo Tilany.[57]

At the end of the night, over 3,000 Gypsies had been murdered. Of the 22,600 Gypsies who entered the Auschwitz Gypsy Camp, at least 19,300 died. Hungarian Jews were moved into the Gypsy Camp, though not for long.

On August 24, the Allies took Paris, led by the Free French tank corps. General de Gaulle entered the city's seat of government, the Hotel de Ville the next day: "Paris outraged, Paris broken, Paris martyred but Paris liberated!"

By the end of the war, Roma and Sinti were in just about all German concentration camps.[58] At the last roll call, on January 13, 1945 there were four Sinti alive in Birkenau. On the 27th of January, the Soviet Army took over the camp.

Resistance in Romania

One should not forget what was done to the Roma, and what the Roma did in Romania.

Romania today is, according to some data sources, the country with the largest Romani population in the world both in terms of numbers and as a percentage of national population. During the 1940s Romania was among the fascist, Nazi-aligned countries that planned to become Gypsy-free, deporting Roma and killing them as part of the Final Solution. Romania was generally aligned with Germany's racial policies. Joseph Goebbels called Romanians "more determined fighters against the Jews than the Germans themselves". [59]Romanian soldiers and police participated in the killing of Jews and Roma. Yet at the war's end, only an estimated 2.5% of Romanian Roma had perished. How so many survived is a remarkable story and is left out of the history education that most Romanians receive.

Romani American scholar Ethel Brooks notes that it can harmful to focus too much on the exciting and heroic tales of those who resisted because it gives the idea that "people who didn't resist were simply quiescent...It doesn't just take an exceptional person to resist; the conditions have to be there." Without laying any blame on those who perished, we should remember the case of Romania because it *is* so exceptional and because it has remained so little recognized.

The anti-minority sentiment sweeping Europe was nothing new to Romania when its dictatorship looked at Germany's racial policies for a model. In 1866, King Carol I took the throne and a new constitution was passed. The new legal framework denied rights to Romanian Jews, making them stateless and encouraging discrimination. Jews did not acquire legal equality there until 1923, and then only briefly. From 1929, the "Jewish question" became increasingly prominent in politics and it was not only the fascist politicians but mainstream parties that exploited anti-Semitic feelings.

After World War One, the Treaty of Versailles returned large territories to Romania and, with them, large Jewish and ethnically non-Romanian communities. Bessarabia, retaken from Russia, was

40-50% Jewish. Half of the original capital of Moldavia, Iasi was Jewish. In 1938, Romania passed anti-Semitic laws based closely on the Nuremberg Laws. When military leader Ioan Antonescu took power, Jews' rights were further reduced with new laws in 1940 and 1941. Half of Romania's Jews would die in the fascist years. As for Roma, even before the War, political voices such as Constantin Papace called for the elimination of both Jews *and* Gypsies. Racial science and eugenics had been going strong in Romanian academia for years and had the attention of General Ion Antonescu.[60] He wrote in 1941, "the principle problem of the nation [*neam*] is race…its salvation…[and] homogenization…" The head of the Central Statistics Institute, Saban Manuila (who had trained, thanks to a grant from the Rockefeller Foundation, at Johns Hopkins University) warned that Roma were the most numerous ethnic group after Romanian and the most "dysgenic".

When the general became dictator, Antonescu gave orders to round up and deport nomadic Gypsies.

Police arrested any Roma who were travelling, treating all Roma on their way to do seasonal farm work away from their home villages as "nomadic". Mirica Dinu grew up in a family that lived in a house but traveled in the summers. "We had tents and carts. We pitched at night and slept there…put down big poles and stretched out a carpet…they were good times, like the Lord's own bread". [61] A passerby might see only dark-skinned savages sleeping under the stars and not see that these were home-owners who spent most of the year like many of their fellow Romanians. They were marked for ethnic cleansing because they enjoyed the heat of summer to travel on holiday or to travel to agricultural areas where short-term, seasonal field labor was in demand.

The May 1942 Order Number 70S/1942, supplemented a few days later by Order 33911, ordered police to survey and round up all Roma and then deport the nomadic ones. Roughly 25,000 people were deported. Orders came to round up non-nomadic Roma as well if they were "dangerous to public order" (order in Report 43249/1942). The legally vague wording allowed, predictably, for some very wide interpretation. When a person sought on the grounds that someone – anyone deemed him "dangerous" was not found, other Roma were arrested in his place. People were often taken because they were home and were Romani while the person sought was away. People were arrested as they went about their day and taken directly to trains for deportation. They went without being allowed to take jackets or bedding, never mind having any sort of judicial hearing.

Although orders were given to issue death certificates when Roma perished en route or in their new homes after deportation, no exact numbers of the dead are known. There were too few gendarmes for accurate record keeping or even enforcement; some Roma fled to Odessa (today in Ukraine) or back into Romania. Many were arrested along the way on their escape routes, were imprisoned elsewhere or died without identification papers.
In Oceakov, entire villages were slaughtered and burnt down. Records of such mass murders were not always kept in careful detail.

Some Roma fled and others physically resisted. Many took to protesting formally, as law-abiding citizens. Even illiterate Roma sent letters to request that their family members who had been taken for deportation might be allowed to come home; those who could not write hired letter writers. Letters insisted that the people deported were not nomadic, were homeowners, had occupations. A Romani gendarme officer wrote to protest the deportation of family members:

"My father fought in World War 1916-18 [*sic*], he has property…lived only by agricultural work. After discussions with the local authorities I think deportation was an error. Please send him home, we are not nomads and do not live by theft, I am a soldier active in the military for my homeland." [62]

Dumitru Marin wrote repeatedly to the authorities on behalf of his deported family: "My relatives are serious people honest home owners…I whose veins flowed the coagulated blood of the holy greater Romania. Even though I am of Gypsy origin, I have lived my whole life a Romanian life…with the obligations and aspirations of the Romanian people. No blame…can justify their deportation to a foreign land...I ask you respectfully with all my soul to remember that in the Great War there were many Gypsy soldiers...they gave their blood for our country..."

The political leadership of the country - fascists and others - showed no concern for the Roma. The Queen Mother Elena did voice disagreement but was not heard by those in politics. A rare and well known exception was the head of the Liberal Party, Constantin Bratianu. In September 1942, he appealed to Antonescu:

"Following the persecutions and expulsions of the Jews as reprisal [Take note here that Bratianu sees the extermination of the Jews as payback or "reprisal", as if the Jews are all guilty of something.] and influenced by German practice, we are now adopting very strict measures against the Gypsies, who are being forcibly removed...They are Orthodox, just like Romanians, and they play an important economic role in our country because they are skilled artisans: blacksmiths, coppersmiths, masons, agricultural workers, construction workers. Many of them are small shopkeepers, small business owners, milkmen and the like. Almost all the violinists in our country are Gypsies and there is not one festival that can go on without their assistance.

"In one fell swoop...[they are removed from] the country in which they were born and where their ancestors lived; the country where, as good Romanians, they shed their blood when fighting for our nation...

Why such cruelty?"[63]

As many Roma fought on the front for their country, deportations of their families went on. Some Roma were arrested and deported even while still wearing their uniforms and on their way to report to duty. Stefan Moise, telling his story decades later, remembered police telling him to "pack your bags" but allowing not a minute to do so. He was taken from his home immediately and loaded onto a freight car.[64] The decision to persecute loyal citizens based on race was neither ethically nor strategically proper. The deportation process tied up transports and put a strain on busy military and police forces.

The deported were sent to Transnistria, where they died quickly under the watchful eye of both Romanian and German militaries. The Ukrainian region had been taken by Germany from the Soviets and put under Romanian control, with much German cooperation. The deportees not massacred faced starvation and disease. According to Jewish survivor Mihail Hausner[65], after 11,500 Roma were killed by the SS in Trihati, the survivors had their possessions confiscated and they were put in the ghetto at Covaleovka. Behind barbed wire, without food, they sold their clothes across the wire. They died, undressed, of hunger and Typhus.

Romani soldiers on leave travelled to Transnistria to find their deported family members. In uniform and armed with military weapons, they brought their relatives home. They did so in increasing numbers. At last, the Supreme General Staff had to ask officers to inform their Romani troops that their families would no longer be deported. In September 1942, the matter was raised at a Council of Ministers meeting:

Mihai Antonescu [Vice President of the Council]: I would like to ask General Vasiliu to discuss this matter with Colonel Davidescu [chief of the dictator's military cabinet] because we have a problem at the national level. Please communicate and transmit a memorandum for enforcement: "All [Gypsies] eligible for military service, their families and who hold a manual trade, smiths, skilled workers, and others do not qualify as evacuees."

Vasiliu [Secretary of State of the Ministry of the Interior]: We brought 26,000…

Alexianu [Governor of Transnistria]: Please give me your approval in case I find Gypsies [in the Army], orphans and invalids from the last war…

Vasiliu: They all have a police file. Are you sending me back all the thieves?

Mihai Antonescu: The ones you arrested, may God protect them, we are not bringing them back.[66]

The Roma in the occupied territory would not all be brought home but the policy would be discontinued. A month later, on October 31 the Ministry of the Interior ended the deportation of Roma to Transnistria. It is hard to imagine how Romani soldiers in Germany or another countries with similar policies could have caused the same reversal. Romania had a mass of Romani military participants that no other country had. Still, it is remarkable that the risk Roma in armed service took, the risk they posed to the system and the change that their actions brought are not better known, even among Roma today.

Rukeli in the Camps

Having recently been cast out of the Wehrmacht, Rukeli was arrested in June 1942. They had come looking for him before and he had hidden each time, sometimes right in plain sight in the apartment, buried in a pile of blankets on his brother's bed. Diana shares the family's pride: "We know that Rukeli sometimes stood up for both Germans and Jews when they were attacked by the SS. He had to hide out in the forest because he knew that the SS were angry...He was so famous here in Hannover that they didn't want to arrest him on the street here. They wanted to take him away quietly. He was a public figure, not so easy for the SS."

Erna Trollmann recalls: "My daughter Elfriede sat as the Gestapo stormed the apartment, on the lap of her uncle. They planned to go fishing. The Gestapo, with big dogs on leashes, went to my brother-in-law. The child clung to her uncle in fear. One of the Gestapo hit the child so hard on the head that she fell unconscious to the floor. As I hurried to help my child, one hit me so hard with a rifle butt in the eye, temple, and back, that I fell to the floor, knocked out." She lost vision in the eye permanently.

She saw Rukeli once more, looking out at her on Hardenberg Street from the window of the Gypsy Central Office. "He waved to me from a window of this house and shouted that I should bring him something to eat, because he'd got nothing."

Carlo, Lolo and Benny went to the office the next day to ask for Rukeli. There was a shouting match. Harms and his colleague, a man named Müller were there. "We're going to make him into soap," Müller said, and warned that they would do the same to his brothers if they did not leave. Still, the managers brought Rukeli out to see his family. His face was battered. His eyes swollen and several teeth were knocked out. Guards carried him, limp. He whispered to Benny to find a pistol and stay away from the Gypsy Central Office.

In October 1942, Johann Trollmann and a truckload of other Roma and Sinti were brought to the Neuengamme Concentration Camp. On arrival, they saw watchtowers, barbed wire and SS guards restraining snarling German Shepherds. The guards shouted at them to move. Prisoners looked weak and starved. Beyond the barracks he had a view of the tall, grey chimneys of the crematorium. An orchestra of prisoners was ordered to perform as new arrivals were led in. The music also played to keep time each morning and night and when dead bodies were carried to the crematorium. The music played when prisoners were whipped as punishment, or hanged or when the dogs were turned on someone.

There were eight barracks in two blocks, a kitchen, and infirmary. There was no slogan over the gate like in Auschwitz. There was, however, an inspirational line written in the kitchen barracks: "There is one way to freedom. Its milestones are called: obedience, diligence, honesty, order, cleanliness, sobriety, truthfulness, sense of sacrifice, and love of Fatherland."

Roll call was long. The prisoners stood and waited for it to end on Rukeli's first day in cold rain. The man next to him wet his pants.

Max Pauly was the camps' commandant. He ran the place with a coterie of men from his hometown, giving out assignments according to his history with people. The camp was not a meritocracy for the prisoners or the guards.

SS Oberführer Albert Lütkemeyer was the highest authority Rukeli saw on his first day. Lütkemeyer had been for years at the camp and worked at Dachau before that. He had seen – no, he had done horrible things. He examined the new arrivals. He would be remembered for searching the pockets of prisoners, always followed by the use of a whip. He laughed and joked at executions. He liked to sing while he hanged prisoners and during the transport of corpses and while watching the dogs maul someone to death. Maybe he needed to maintain bravado to keep going or, then again, maybe he was the total sadist that survivors of the camp would recall. If not, he played the part convincingly.

Addressing the new residents, he advised them: "Prepare yourself to be lowered and humiliated. You are entering a new world…If you have a wife, children, relatives or friends in the outside world, then forget them as you will never see them again. And forgetting, that can I assure you, is much easier for your peace of mind."[67]

Rukeli may have looked a bit different since the beating at the Gypsy Central Office. He may have looked different since the days of good nutrition and daily training. Still, he could assume that the Oberführer would recognize him soon enough because Albert Lütkemeyer had been a boxing referee. While Rukeli knew to keep silent, he must have wondered whether the brotherhood of boxing would mean anything here and if recognition could help him.

Rukeli was neither the only boxer in Neuengamme nor the only prisoner whose name can hold meaning for today's reader. Vladimir Nabokov's brother, Sergei was kept there as well as Fritz Pfeffer, one of the Jews who lived under the same roof with Anne Frank.

Top boxers were interned in several camps. Victor "Young" Perez, the Tunisian-born Jew and world champion would be taken to Auschwitz. Other young prisoners learned the sport by fighting under duress for the amusement of the guards. Polish Jew Harry Haft,[68] who would eventually immigrate to America and fight professionally against such competitors as Rocky Marciano, was one such case.

Rukeli and the other inmates were taken to a building with group showers, given soap and directed to stand and wait for water. It was always freezing or burning. They were brought to be shaven. Sitting naked in rows, the prisoners had their hair removed; first heads, then legs and crotches, then they were covered in anti-lice powder. Finally, used clothes were distributed.

Clothes that fit were rare. Outfits could be absurd as people were handed whatever was left behind by past residents of the camp. Someone in Rukeli's group found himself in a tuxedo jacket with tails.

Rukeli and other Gypsies then had to sew on their identifying patches. There was a patch with a Z for *Zigeuner* and a number. His was 9841. Prisoners were instructed not to use their own or one another's names. Some prisoners would later recall that even being called by a number was less common than "dog", "bitch" or other insults.

New prisoners had ten days in quarantine and there were taught the rules. Don't go within three meters of the Kommandoführer. This was punishable by beatings with a hose to the head. Clothes were washed every 8-12 weeks. Prisoners were not allowed to wash their own clothing. Jews, Gypsies and Poles were to wait at lunchtime until others had been served. If food had not run out, they would have what was left over. Until 1941, the camp had only held people from Germany. Now there were others; Dutch, Belgians, and French.

Having been taught the rules, a prisoner was ready to begin labor. The camp was an SS-owned brick factory, a private but SS-owned commercial enterprise. By the end of the war, the SS owned more than forty companies with around 150 factories and businesses. The SS operated in lines of business like stones and earth, food and drink, wood and iron works, agriculture, forestry, textile and leather working, and even publishing.

The brickworks contributed to the development of nearby Hamburg, which Hitler wanted to make into a "calling card of National Socialism." Albert Speer was to direct the redesign. Hamburg paid for the construction of transportation ways: the city agreed to build a canal from the Dove-Elbe to the works, and to construct a loading berth and a train siding to the works. The transport of the stones by train was also to be paid for by the city. The costs for these projects were estimated low because "the Reich offers…prisoners as laborers and the necessary guard teams for use for free." Stone production in 1942 was, and had been for some time, under its promise of 200 million stones per year.

Eventually other companies would be allowed to access Neuengamme's slave labor and the bricks would take lower priority than war-essential production. Walther-Werke built a finishing station for weapon manufacture. The Deutsche Messapparate-GmbH Langenhorn, or "Messap" built a factory for detonators for anti-aircraft shells. One hundred forty prisoners worked there with tweezers and magnifying glasses. Others worked on submarine motors and on speedboats.

Production needed workers and more and more prisoners were brought from other camps. By the end of 1942, the camp was severely crowded with a population of 5,000. The wood and stone barracks had bunk beds three levels high and there were usually two people per bed. On arrival, Rukeli shared his bed with another Sinto. He died a few days later, shot for trying to escape. It is not known whether the man was in fact making a run for it. Guards sometimes order prisoners to go fetch something over the fence and shot the prisoners while they were following the order.

Rukeli saw cruelty every day. One Kapo laid boards over a waterway and commanded prisoners to run with fully loaded wheelbarrows over them. The planks were slippery. If people fell in, they could drown. Even if no prisoner fell, sometimes the Kapo shook the boards until one did. The guards did not encourage Kapos to be likeable. They misdirected hate from the guards but only if provoked to be especially worthy of the anger.

As in Auschwitz, Gypsies were used for medical experiments, including testing with typhus. It is not known what Rukeli saw or knew of these experiments.

Rations became smaller as the workforce grew. From mid-1942 to September 1943, the prisoner numbers went from 3,000 to 10,000. The camps were a study in the madness of competing and mutually exclusive goals. The aim of extracting productive labor from prisoners was at obvious odds with the process of killing prisoners through unendurable conditions. One man ate his daily ration and, still hungry, swallowed a glass of syrup that he had somehow acquired and hidden. He could not keep it down. When he vomited, a Pole watching from nearby ran over to eat it from the floor.[69]

In winter, they were ordered to begin attending roll call naked, for better inspection. Rukeli and the others stood under falling snow and shook as the count was shouted. If someone fell, other prisoners held him up. There were consequences for showing the inability to follow the rules and to stand at attention.

Prisoners died at a steady pace in Neuengamme and its annexed camps in 1943, usually from starvation and related illnesses. People fought over potato peels. Others discovered earthworms to eat in the grounds near their barracks. Rukeli, like many, was usually sick. He developed bloody diarrhea. He must have seen others with it and known how close he was to death.

There were Romani and Sinti children in the camp, some born there and many orphans. They were dispatched to clean the camp streets in the morning, as soon as the adults had moved off.

One morning as these children were going about their duties, Lütkemeyer called out Prisoner 9841 as the inmates were dispersing after roll call. He asked if the prisoner wasn't once a professional boxer. Yes, Rukeli said. Lütkemeyer told him to report in the evening to the SS camp, to train some of the guards. He would receive food. And his work assignment changed. He was to work in the day in the garden, where salad vegetables were raised for the SS.

He would have energy for the evenings. And he would be clean and disease free. His Kapo informed him that he would have new clothes and be allowed to shower. No lice or typhus would enter the SS camp.

He was even greeted with a shot of schnapps before starting the first training. He went slowly, showed the men the correct stance, how to move the head away from a blow, to keep one's hands up. He worked with them for an hour and when it was over, the men gave him some bread. Reaching his barracks, he kept part for himself and handed some out to children and friends.

On the second night, the guards wanted to try sparring. He put on gloves and worked with them. He was too weak to do much but get hit. The session over, he was sent back to his barracks with a black eye and more bread.

Boxing fans are at times asked to defend the sport. What is the difference between boxing and violence, people ask? Boxing lovers will offer an endless list of arguments. Ultimately, the distinction between the martial sport and violence is as clear and great as the distance between sex and rape. It is consent. Boxers choose to box. How the spectators feel about the idea of hurting and being struck and injured is irrelevant. Violence is not a process of mutual consent, ended at any moment by either party. Boxing is a sport because one willfully participates, a sport one embraces despite or even because of the suffering that it demands. Rukeli was not the only inmate forced to don gloves in the concentration camps. None of this was boxing. He took the abuse because he had no choice and took the payment of a piece of bread for the same reason.

Christmas was not celebrated in the camp. In some blocks, the prisoners sang but not in Rukeli's barracks.

On New Year's Eve boxing training was cancelled along with much of the usual routine. The SS had a little bit of a party and got drunk. It was a time to relax. They tied prisoners to a whipping bench and made a game of flogging them.

Trollmann's diarrhea continued and he gained no weight. He received no medical care. He had a damaged rib from sparring. Still, he had to go to boxing training every day if he wanted to get his bread and to stay in the garden in the daytime.

In February, work began on the Dove-Elbe. If someone fell down in the cold frost from fatigue, the SS poured buckets of water on their heads, letting them freeze to death.

Rukeli might as well have died like that. He lacked the will and the strength to go on. He told people in the barracks he would not show up for training any more. They pushed him. Go and bring back bread for the children, they urged.

On February Seventh he threw some punches, tried to show that he had some life in him. Guards put him in his place. He returned to the barracks with a bleeding, broken nose. He was dejected and again said that he would not go back.

On the Ninth of February he was listed as dead in the records. His cause of death was written as "various heart and circulatory weaknesses, bronchopneumonia". The death certificate was witnessed, meaning it was co-signed by a criminal prisoner, Otto Appenburg, who had little alternative to signing whatever was presented to him. The time of death was listed as six a.m. Time of death at Neuengamme was always an approximation, listed as on the hour or five, ten, or fifteen minutes past. In the morgue, golden fillings were removed. The corpse identified as Johann Trollmann's had three fillings that, like all gold, were removed, melted and became property of the SS.

The teeth were not Rukeli's and he was not dead.

Though prisoners were not allowed to organize in any way, there was a secret prisoners' committee, led by a charismatic twenty-three year old Belgian named André Mandryxcs. (Official records at times list him as Mandryx, Mandrycks and by several other spellings and are equally inconsistent about his nationality, sometimes listing him as French.) The committee decided that Rukeli's loss was both a terrible blow to the morale of the Gypsies in the camp and to many others. On the night of the 8th, members of the committee approached Rukeli with a new way to fight. They let him in on their plan to deny the SS the opportunity to slap him around. Identities were exchanged. Rukeli's clothes and badge were swapped with those of a dead man who also had three fillings. Rukeli's death was reported by a prisoner to an SS officer. The body of "Johann Trollmann" was cremated.

The Trollmann family was billed for the incineration and funeral. The family went on a warm day in March to see the burial of Rukeli's urn in Ricklingen. Mourners talked about conditions in the camp. If a strong person like Rukeli died in a few months, what must the conditions be? Who could survive there? Rumors circulated that the government intended to kill all the Sinti. There were many people who knew well what was happening inside the camps and yet others did not know or could not bring themselves to believe what they heard. Some Sinti, like many of the Trollmanns, hoped that the worst stories were only a product of awful imaginations. Still, they knew they were meant for incarceration in the camps. People looked over their shoulders, worried that police would use the funeral as a chance to round them all up. Rukeli's mother and sisters cried as his urn was buried and as the committee put the living Rukeli into hiding. A Blockführer and a couple Kapos were in on the plan. Political prisoners and criminals worked together to nurse him and keep him out of sight for a couple days. He was fed and put on some weight. A new badge, with the red markings of a political prisoner, was found for him.

Transports were leaving often for sub-camp Wittenberge an der Elbe, where 28,000 captives were held. The collaborators found a way to sneak him on board a train. Wittenberge was one of around sixty sub-camps that were built in the area near Neuengamme.

At Wittenberge, a Sinto named Rudolf Landsberger, originally from Amsterdam recognized Rukeli and embraced him.

At this same time, Jan Yoors, now twenty years old, was held and being interrogated in a Nazi-run facility in France. His metal cell door opened and guards led him to an interrogation room where another prisoner's questioning was ending. The naked victim was facedown, strapped on a narrow rack suspended over two wooden horses. Germans drank beer and chatted as the guards removed him, holding him up by the armpits and walking him from the room. He lost bladder control as he was dragged away. Yoors was told that the Nazis knew all about his activities and that, one way or another, he would confess and give up whatever information they wanted. The torture began.

Back at Wittenberge, there were 150 to 200 people per barracks. Work there ran smoothly, prisoners going every day to a factory just 150 meters away. Rukeli was now, like his new barracks mates, under Commandant Kierstein, a small man of fifty-three years who was not satisfied letting Kapos and men under his command beat prisoners. He liked to participate personally, at times beating people to death.

He kept a pet cat named Minka and liked to feed it well in front of hungry prisoners. People called him Commandant Minka.

Rukeli went to work doing some of the hardest tasks in the camp. He unloaded, stacked and transported straw bales with thirty to forty other prisoners. Things were hard but not more frightening than in Neuengamme. There was no smell of burning corpses. Prisoners washed once per month. In 1943, water was installed in the kitchen and washroom barracks, though it did not often work. Nutrition began to improve along with production. Rukeli slept, like before, in an unheated barracks but the coldest nights of the year were past and he now had a bed to himself.

In France, Yoors's captors were sure there was nothing left to extract from him. One day, with no explanation, he was walked to the prison gate and told to go. He expected to be shot for "attempting escape" as he moved toward the exit. And then he was on the street.

He made his way to Brussels, where he contacted a Sinti family he had met years before. What he knew of the Sinti was mostly hearsay from the Lowara. Sinti did not have arranged marriages, he had heard. Lowara looked down on this and doubted that Sinti women had the same morality as Romani wives. Still, the family who took him in did all they could for him, fully aware of the risks of bringing him into their home. He ate his first real meal in months, "in the privacy of a home…surrounded by warm concerned people and numerous affectionate children… an unforgettable feast. We ate thick potato pancakes, sauerkraut, and a providential, heaven-sent pig's stomach."[70] His host Tikno and his wife, Poffi had information about the Lowara and Tchurara. Many of the groups hiding with the partisans had been captured. They had been taken to concentration camps.

Rukeli's conditions did not improve. In April 1944 a British bomber plane appeared over Wittenberg. Six bombs came down, killing civilians and two prisoners in the camp. The hay burned. Guards and prisoners alike knew that the end of the war was close. In September there was a second bomb attack. The Commandant, Kierstein was killed. As American and British bombs became common over

Germany, Goebbels assured the public: "A people, who until this point have only boxed with the left and have yet to wrap up the right [Boxers wrap their hands before putting on gloves.] and use it ruthlessly in the next round, have no reason to be yielding."

A camp elder arranged a fight to entertain some prisoners. Rukeli was told that he would fight with a Kapo, Emil Cornelius. Cornelius was a criminal and had been a prisoner since 1936. He was from eastern Prussia and spoke with a distinctive accent.

Tired men clapped to cheer the opponents. The fight was short. People laughed as Rukeli drove the Kapo back, struggling to protect his face. Rukeli hit him in the nose and knocked him off of his feet. Again, people cheered and laughed. The humiliation was not forgotten.

Soon, the German went back from boxing opponent to Kapo and had control over the Gypsy. Cornelius was in charge of Rukeli and Landsberger as the three of them worked to stack heavy bales of hay.

Cornelius beat Rukeli with his Kapo's club, fatally striking him on the head. He reported the death to be an accident and made Landsberger hold his tongue.

Most Sinti and Roma perished as numbers in the camps. They were anonymous deaths, stripped of personhood. Rukeli died because of who he was. He was killed for being the Sinto boxer that so many white opponents could not defeat. He was interred in the ground there at Wittenberge.

Historians debate the total number of Roma and Sinti whose lives were taken during the years of genocide. 500,000 is the most quoted figure but many believe it to be a severe undercounting. At the first U.S. Conference on Romani people in the Holocaust, at Drew University in November, 1995 Sybil Milton, senior historian at the U.S. Holocaust Research Institute (the US Holocaust Memorial Museum) stated: "We believe that something between half a million and a million and a half Romanies were murdered in Nazi Germany and occupied Europe between 1939 and 1945."[71]

Protestors, Soldiers and Partisans

Rukeli and the other Sinti and Roma who struck back at racism in the preceding pages were remarkable but not alone.

In many countries and in many ways, Roma collaborated in discreet and dangerous efforts to stop the Nazi military machine and its partners.

Along the border of Albania, the Romani partisans of Yugoslavia's 19th Brigade fought the fascists.

In Slovakia, Roma took great risk by assisting the anti-Nazi partisan fighters. Resistance fighters came to Romani villages seeking food and supplies as well as help getting familiar with the terrain and with other intelligence. This support went on even as Nazis tortured and killed Roma suspected of working with the partisans.

Men who looked like partisans came to the village of Tisovec, Slovakia and asked if any of the Romani men would join them in blowing up a nearby bridge. When some of the men agreed, the "partisans" revealed themselves to be SS officers. Everyone present in the village, forty-four men, women and children were exterminated and the village was burned down. Such things happened in Romani communities across the Axis and Nazi-occupied countries.[72]

The entire forty-five person population of the Romani village of Lutila, Slovakia was killed on suspicion of being resistors. A woman whose father was mayor when this occurred would later say to interviewing historians: "The Gypsies weren't bad…They didn't steal…when they were taking them away, my father had to be there and they fell on their knees and begged, 'Mr. Mayor, save us. Mr. Mayor, save us. But he said, 'What can I do?'"[73]

Anna Conkova, a Romani whose brother was one of the partisans (and was eventually shot) recalls: "One evening, three partisans came to our settlement…one such evil-doer…went to the Germans to inform them that my brother was drinking with the partisans. And so the Germans came at night and captured those partisans. They lit a fire, tied them...and turned them over that fire. They burned them alive...the Germans came to us. 'Who has a gun?'.... They grabbed my dad – he had just had surgery – stuck a rifle into him. Dad's wound opened.... I might have been twelve years old...they chased us all out of our huts, lined us up." A white farmer came and pleaded with the Germans not to shoot them all. How would he go on with no farmhands, he implored? The farmer proved more capable than the mayor in the story above. The Roma survived. The freedom fighters returned that same night to the village and the Roma gave them bread loaves, matches and tobacco.

In some countries, Roma were viewed – and killed – as resistors whether they fought the Nazis or not. In 1942, the German forces in the Soviet Union saw all Roma as anti-fascist. Local military commander Norwoshew shot 128 Roma because there had been an order from Field Commander 822 that "Gypsies are always to be treated as partisans". [74] In Belarus too, orders for Operation Hamburg stated that: "every bandit Jew, Gypsy...is to be regarded as an enemy". Albert Rapp, the head of the Sonderkommando 7am, which killed Gypsies in Smolensk in 1942, gave testimony decades later when tried for war crimes. He described shooting Romani women and children in 1942. Though it was cold, the victims were forced to strip their clothes first and to stand, shivering and waiting. Mothers were made to carry their babies to a ditch that was to be used as a mass grave. The killers took the babies, held them up and shot them in the neck before tossing them into the ditch. This was standard practice. A Secret Field Police report explained that all the Roma must be killed because "if only those who are suspected or convicted of helping the partisans were to be punished, the remainder would become still more hostile toward the German forces...necessary that such bands be exterminated mercilessly".

In Soviet Crimea, the Roma had generally lived settled lives for generations. When the Germans began to slaughter them, a report was requested on how the activity would affect local attitudes to the occupiers. The report advised that the killing of Gypsies and Krimchaks (a local tribe classified as Jewish) along with Jews caused no strong concern in the local population. With so little care for their lives among the non-Roma, some Gypsies found the courage to stand up for themselves.

Alfreda Markowska would not have seemed the most likely heroine at the start of life. Born in a caravan to a travelling Romani family in Poland (in an area that is now within Ukraine), she was arrested by the Germans in Lviv in 1939. Her siblings, parents and entire clan were massacred on the outskirts of Biala Podlaska in 1941. She was the sole survivor, an orphan at age fifteen. Alfreda stayed in the woods for days, alone and without food, looking for her family's mass grave. She was married at sixteen and, not long after, both she and her husband were arrested by the Ukrainian police. The police turned them over to the Germans. They were sent to ghettoes in Lublin, Lodz and Belzec.

They escaped from each place. Living outside of ghettoes or camps and knowing the consequences of being caught, Alfreda still did not make her own safety her priority. She went wherever pogroms or mass killings were known to have happened and collected any surviving children. She brought fifty Jewish and Romani children back to her home, helping them through a small network of resistors to hide, obtain false papers and stay away from the Germans' hands until the end of the war.

Acts of heroism during Europe's darkest moments were not rare. It is the awareness of these acts that is lacking.

Aftermath

By the end of the Nazi's rule most German Roma and Sinti went into the concentration camps. Ninety percent died. An even higher percentage of Roma and Sinti in the Sudetenland and the Protectorate of Bohemia and Moravia perished. There are Roma today in the Czech Republic almost entirely as a result of movement from Slovakia within 1950s and 1960s Czechoslovakia. In many of the countries that came under fascist control, the genocide came very close to complete success.

The map of Europe was, in the post-war period, less ethnically and linguistically diverse than before the upheaval. We often read that the Nazis *almost* succeeded; we overlook that they *did* succeed in wiping several cultural-linguistic communities from the map. The Sinti community of the Czech lands and Moravia, by example, is gone. Fascism did not put an end to the Jews but it did permanently extinguish some Jewish communities and cultures. At the beginning of the twentieth century, the majority of people in Thessaloniki were Ladino-speaking, Sephardic Jews. Thessaloniki, which had been home to Jews since the days when Paul the Apostle visited them, was cleansed of this heritage. After the war, several countries forced their ethnic German populations to leave. Czechoslovakia marched thousands of Germans to the German border and expelled them. German linguistic communities in places as far apart as Croatia and Ukraine vanished. The end of the Second World War did not mean an immediate end to ethnic homogenization by forced migration.

Some of the leaders of the fascist mass murder were punished. Many more were not. The Romanian dictator, Ian Antonescu was interrogated in 1946; he defended himself and his government, claiming that Romanians were victims of foreign propaganda aimed at making it look like Romania was a "country full of Roma".[75]

Leni Riefenstahl's film using Sinti and Roma prisoners as extras, *Lowlands* took years to complete but was finally released in 1954. It was a terrible flop. Riefenstahl, according to critics, was not a convincing Gypsy temptress. Up against masterpiece films released in the same year such as *La Strada, Lowlands* was swept under the carpet and forgotten.

Members of the Ritter Institute, responsible for so much of the Reich's racial science and policy toward the Roma and Sinti were investigated but *none* were put on trial. By Ritter's own account, the racial assessments he and the Institute developed were to provide data "for the measures taken by the state in the areas of eugenics and racial hygiene". In other words, ethnic cleansing was the expressed purpose of his work. Sinti remain even today distrustful of anthropology and all social scientists.

Emil Cornelius, the Kapo who beat Rukeli to death went on to commit other crimes. It is said that he once threw a live grenade into a room full of prisoners. He was never punished for these acts. He did serve other prison sentences after the war, from 1947 to 1961 for other crimes.

Harns and Muller, the two policemen who beat Rukeli at the Gypsy Central Office in 1942 before his departure to Neuengamme, were never made to answer for their crimes in any court and enjoyed long lives. Wilhem, Rukeli's older brother and one of just two brothers to survive the war once paid one of the ex-policemen a visit at home according to his great grand-daughter, and "you know, he told him a few things". Small acts can bring a lasting sense of redemption.

In the last days before the Allied invasion of the area, the military commanders of Hamburg and its surroundings believed it would be easier to face their captors if the concentration camp prisoners were not around to tell the stories of their mistreatment. Surviving prisoners of Neuengamme were loaded onto ships and taken out to sea. There, the British bombed the ships, unable to know about the boats' prisoner cargo. On one ship 4,500 prisoners died. On another, three thousand perished. While records show that Andre Mandrycks died in the camp on May 3, 1945 and was buried there, some researchers believe that the records are incorrect and that the leader of the plot to rescue Rukeli was among those who died at sea.[76]

Neuengamme was used by the British military, after the Allied arrival, as a temporary prison for Germans accused of war crimes.

Armand Stenegry, the French Manouche who led fellow Gypsy partisans on missions at Normandy was awarded medals by both the British and the French militaries. In 1965 he recorded several church hymn for the growing Gypsy evangelical church, written to score that Django Reinhardt had composed.

Django died of a cerebral hemorrhage on May 16th 1953, the anniversary of the Romani uprising at Auschwtiz-Birkenau, at the age of forty-three. His coffin was brought down the cobblestone streets of Samois, his final home to the town's medieval church for a ceremony and burial. In the Manouche tradition, the family vacates the deceased's caravan and burns it with all the lost person's worldly possessions. Django's guitar went up in flames. His name was not to be used again. According to custom, he was the first and last Manouche of his name.

Poffi, the Sinti woman who hosted Jan Yoors in Brussels was taken off by the Germans after one of her grandchildren turned her in. Desperate to be accepted as a member of the human race by boys his own age, the boy was temporarily admitted to the Hitler Youth and shared his grandparents' address to show his loyalty to the group. Her husband Tikno, who was not home when the soldiers came, survived.

Jan Yoors became an artist. He passed away but his photography (including photos of Romani friends in this book) and artwork continue to be shown in exhibits in Europe and the United States.

Alfreda Markowska, the Romani teenage girl who saved so many Romani and Jewish children was recognized by Polish President Kaczynski in 2006 and awarded Poland's Commander's Cross with a Star of the Order of Polonia Restituta in honor of her heroism.

Many of Pulika's Lowara partisans in France were eventually captured and sent to Auschwitz and other camps. Those who lived worked through Yoors after the war to see what promises from the

Resistance could be fulfilled. They learned that no offer of amnesty or other recognition of their risks had been duly authorized and none would be forthcoming.

Among the survivors of the resistance movement, experiences were life-shaping even if rarely discussed. Yoors' son, Kore visited an old woman in Belgium, a friend of his father's. It was decades after the war and after Jan's passing. As they exchanged information on how to reach others in the old network, Kore noticed that the woman wrote her notes on inconveniently tiny scraps of paper. He asked her why. "I only write names and phone numbers on paper small enough to quickly chew and swallow," explained the elderly hostess.

Many of France's Roma and Manouche, held in concentration camps during the war, were not released upon the war's end. The de Gaulle government took fifteen months to finally release the Gypsies detained in the Montreuil-Bellay camp, for example. They were ultimately let go so that the camp could detain other civilians accused of no crime – ethnic Germans from France's Alsace.

When the United States entered the war, many of the country's professional boxers, including Max Baer, entered military service. The Jewish presence in American boxing ended almost overnight. The great majority of those who left the sport to serve their country never returned to the ring. Some found they had taken too much time from training. Others took advantage of the GI Bill, went to college and embarked on new careers. Younger men, again mostly from minority communities filled their ranks in the boxing gyms.

Max Baer stayed in the public limelight for years. In 1959, he refereed a televised fight in Phoenix, Arizona, jumping over the ropes and into the ring to applause. The next day, he drove to Hollywood for the filming of a television commercial. He chatted with hotel employees at the front desk as he checked into his hotel. Two days later, he called the front desk and asked for a doctor. He was having chest pains. The desk clerk assured him that "a house doctor would be right up." "A house doctor?" he joked. "No, dummy, I need a people doctor." While being attended to by the doctor and while mentioning casually that he had recently had similar attacks, he turned blue. "Oh

God, here I go." He turned on his side and died minutes later, aged fifty. At his funeral, the pallbearers included Joe Louis and Jack Dempsey. He left behind three children. Max Baer, Jr. is best known for playing Jethro on *The Beverly Hillbillies*.

While boxing had not been a clean sport, free of organized crime's interests before the war, American gangsters took an even stronger role in the 1940s. Prominent mobsters who were also boxing promoters included, notably, Frankie Carbo (born Paolo Carbo) of Murder Incorporated and the Lucchese crime family. Some people believe that Carbo is responsible for Bugsy Siegel's murder. Among his close partners were Meyer Lanksy's associate and former boxer Harry "Champ" Segal and a surrounding group of fight fixers who sometimes called themselves The Combination. Carbo and other members of The Combination controlled the contract of 1950s heavyweight champion Sonny Liston and of many other top talents.

In Europe, Jews continued to populate boxing halls in countries where they were among the struggling poor refugees in the war's aftermath. Robert Cohen of France (born in colonial Algeria) held the World Bantam Championship title from 1954 to 1956. Alphonse Halimi, also a Jew who arrived in *metropole* France from Algeria held the same title from 1957 to 1959. Even in Europe, most Jews would soon pass from poverty and, at the same time, from boxing.

Erich Seelig, the Jewish boxer who trained Rukeli and who became light-heavyweight champion before he was forced to leave his home country received, like Rukeli, some posthumous recognition. In 2006, the American Association for the Improvement of Boxing presented his son and widow with the Rocky Marciano AAIB Champions Award.

Hitler tired of Schmeling's reluctance to join the Nazi party and had him drafted into the Luftwaffe's elite paratroopers, a job that meant near certain death. Schmeling survived the war nonetheless and outlived Hitler. Retiring from boxing, he went to work for Coca-Cola in post-war Germany and developed a social relationship with Joe Louis. He died in 2005, at the age of 99.

Landsberger, Rukeli's fellow Sinto prisoner gave testimony after the war regarding Rukeli's time at Wittenberge and his murder. In 1970, Rukeli's grave at Ricklingen-Hannover was leveled and his name removed, given it is not where his remains were buried.

In 1989, Romani immigrants to West Germany, mostly from Yugoslavia, gathered with German Roma at the site of the Neuengamme camp to demand more welcoming immigration policies and to protest planned expulsions. Even as West Germany took in increasing numbers of white East German migrants, the country turned away Roma from Yugoslavia and across the Communist bloc.[77]

Led by Hamburg-based Romani community organizer Rudko Kawczynski, who was born in Nazi-occupied Poland, an estimated forty adults and thirty young people marched with police escorts from the concentration camp where Rukeli and so many others were tormented, to Hamburg. Meanwhile, hundreds more occupied a site at the former concentration camp. Deputy Mayor of Hamburg, Ingo von Munch disapproved: "I believe there must be one taboo. A former concentration camp must never be misused for political demands by any group." The deputy mayor may have been unaware of the many ways that the Holocaust is interpreted and presented by so many governments and political leaders, but it is hard to imagine. By 1989, Roma and Sinti had learned painful lessons in how memory and the overlooking of facts about the Holocaust always carry both political and personal impacts.

In an early chapter, the reader finds Rukeli at a boxing hall, seeing a shower for the first time. Europe has developed, yet the Europe in which many Roma live has not. The mention of Rukeli's first exposure to a shower reminds Jud Nirenberg of his experience in the 1990s in Hungary. He had organized a seminar to help Romani community leaders learn skills for political activism. People from small Romani villages and slums across Hungary came to the hotel, where they would stay for a three-day training schedule. On the first night, a father and man of considerable influence in his community came to the author, then a young man wet behind the ears, to shyly ask that they go up to his room together and see something. They took an elevator full of low-budget travelers; graduate students and backpackers whose lives were incoherently far rom the experiences of the trainees. They arrived at the tidy room with its freshly painted white walls, a TV hanging in the corner and a remote control on a little desk. "Brother," the older man said in Romani, "come show me how to use this thing." He opened the bathroom door and pointed at the shower. Unlike white Hungarians who had cable TV and air conditioning, the Rom was not used to running water in his home.

The Jews, for the most part, departed central and eastern Europe after the genocide. The same opportunities for mass migration were not opened to Roma, who stayed in the same ghettoes, within societies with many of the same old biases and obstacles to integration.

Near Berlin's Brandenburg Gate, visitors today may see a memorial designed by the Israeli artist Dani Karavan, dedicated to all the Roma and Sinti murdered in the 1930s and 1940s. In painted letters around the edge of the pool is the poem *Auschwitz* by Romani poet Santino Spinelli:

Gaunt face
dead eyes
cold lips
quiet
a broken heart
out of breath
without words
no tears

Memorials or even public mentions of the Roma and Sinti who died are few.

The Trollmanns who survived carries stories of the loved ones who did not. Not all of the family can bear to talk about the past but several have put Holocaust memory - as well as current human rights issues - at the center of their lives. When Rukeli's nephew was first interviewed for this book, he could not wait to ask the American writer about Guantanamo and other international rights issues. An acute compassion and concern about how human beings treat one another is the Trollmann family legacy. They are also a proudly educated family. As Diana Ramos-Farina, Rukeli's grand-niece says proudly, "We all have an occupation." She studied English and is in academia. Her father works in renewable energy. Another relative works at the local courthouse.

In December 2003, Rukeli's brother Ferdinand and great nephew Manuel Trollmann received, on Rukeli's behalf, a champion's belt from the German Boxing Association. Johann Trollmann was recorded as the 1933 German champion after a fight, as Repplinger puts it, of seventy years and two rounds.

On the 24th of August, 2004, Tiefenthal Street in Hannover was renamed Johann Trollmann Way. The renaming of the street was also the culmination of a long fight. Rukeli's use of the ring as a setting for anti-racist statement was only one of many ways that Roma, Sinti, and others pushed back against bigotry and oppression.

Discrimination and Exclusion After the War

Sinti and Roma across Europe died in German-run death camps during the war. Some were exempted from deportation to the camps after being sterilized; the Nazi plan was not to murder every single Gypsy in the camps but was to end the Roma and the Sinti as a "race" within a generation. The plan evolved, becoming more aggressive and thorough over time. Recognition that there was a plan to exterminate the Roma and Sinti as ethnic groups, however, did not come immediately upon the end of fascism. Raphael Lemkin, the man credited with first using the word *genocide*, described Roma as being victims of Nazi genocide along with Jews in a 1951 speech but others would take much longer to agree.[78]

After the war, a Germany occupied by the victors had to confront its collective sins. The German people were confronted and its people educated, by the new West German and East German governments and by foreign powers, of the evils of anti-Semitism. Old prejudices and practices toward Roma and Sinti, however, were not immediately condemned.

In the early 1950s, a West German professional police journal published an analysis of the "racial purity" of Gypsies in the country, worrying that only about 20% were "racially pure Gypsies" and supposing this to have implications for Gypsies' behavior.[79]

Even earlier, in 1946 authorities in Hannover complained to the military about Gypsies in the area who had returned from camps, homeless. "For Gypsies, special measures are required" said the Hannover representative. They were not, apparently, to be treated like other citizens in socio-economic despair. In 1948, the official responsible for compensation of Holocaust victims in North Rhineland-Westphalia's Ministry of Interior, Dr. Marcel Frenkel found it necessary, as Roma and Sinti were not receiving the same treatment as other victims, to send a letter to the Presidents of Administrative Headquarters explaining: "Gypsies and Gypsies of mixed blood fall under the category of racially persecuted and are to be treated according to those guidelines…I request that you process all the applications currently pending accordingly."[80] He needed to remind of the rules because, in fact, they were not being applied. His letter did not settle the matter.

Failure to properly give Roma and Sinti benefits available to victims of Nazi persecution was not the worst discrimination in post-war West Germany. The mayor of Grafenhausen, who had been active in the deportation of Gypsies in 1940, wrote in official government correspondence in 1952: "I am strictly opposed to allowing the Gypsies to resettle anywhere near the village limits...citizens of this community must fight hard for their daily bread. Gypsies just want to feed themselves at the expense of others." To make the exact same statement in West Germany, replacing the word *Gypsies* with *Jews*, would have been unfathomable.

In 1953, Bavarian law required "vagrants" – in practice, mostly Roma – to carry passes and report frequently to the police. Even more extreme, there was a drive in the 1950s in North Rhine-Westphalia to strip Roma of their German nationality.

One should not be shocked by the continuity of norms from before the Allied occupation. Even though there was an intense foreign drive to confront the German people with the horrors of what Nazi-led Germany had done, many of the old civil servants remained in place. In the 1950s it was estimated that 60% of public servants in Bavaria, for example, were known former Nazis.[81] Occupiers in the early years were often surprised to find their old enemies had become their partners and that Western powers overlooked criminal pasts in return for cooperation.[82]

A law existed in West Germany since 1945 for the compensation of victims of Nazism who had been mistreated for religious, racial or political motives. A 1955 commentary on the law by senior officials in the Compensation Authority gave guidelines to the public officials implementing the law: "Since the beginning of time, the Gypsies have been regarded by Western civilized nations as a state plague....the Gypsies' character...wandering drive...were occasion for combatting them." In other words, Roma and Sinti had deserved the Nazi policies are deserved no compensation.[83]

Even those who put themselves forward as the kind helpers of the Gypsies could hold and express views that were less than enlightened. The vicar Georg Althaus tried to help Roma and Sinti in Holocaust compensation claims. In the 1950s, he was in charge of the Evangelical Lutheran Church's Mission to Israel and for the Gypsies, and was the founder of the Lutheran Gypsy mission. He wrote, "Let us stop trying to re-fashion the Gypsies. Otherwise, we will lose them. Better to let the Gypsies be Gypsies and develop naturally into true Gypsies…" In another paper, he argued that Gypsies had always lied, stolen and wandered and that, in spite of it, Jesus loved them. He questioned: "whether they don't also have loveable traits". With friends like these, what sort of respect and equality could Roma and Sinti expect from society as a whole?

Roma and Sinti in the early post-war period had few advocates. They certainly needed more voices to join them in seeking recognition as people equal to other Germans, and equal to other victims of the Third Reich. Those who sought victims' benefits generally did so, in the 1950s through the 1970s, on their own, with neither the assistance of an organization dedicated to their concerns nor strong public interest in their small minority community. They were simply not backed by the same powers as were other claimants to restitution. *Wiedergutmachung*, or "making good again", as officials called compensation, was a complex and expensive process for the West Germans. The word *Wiedergutmachung*, coined by the German Jewish exile Siegfried Moses in Israel in 1943, came to encompass payments the West German government made to individuals, to other countries including Israel and to organizations representing victims' ethnic communities. (East Germany showed no interest in making good; Socialism was the enemy of fascism and so Eastern Bloc states had no responsibility for the sins their citizens or even political officials had committed a few years prior.)

In the early years, the Roma and Sinti of Germany had neither a country nor an organization to stand behind their claims. In all, the Germans paid heavily to other victim groups in the initial years after the war. Until the 1960s, between 2.5% and 5.5% of the national annual budget and the German federal states' budgets were going to compensation. Since 1980, compensation has made up around 0.5%

of federal spending. The Swiss government and some private companies that benefitted from slave labor organized by the Third Reich have also paid into compensation funds. Roma and Sinti did, in the early years, receive some restitution but very little given their numbers. In light of the prejudices and given the huge sums being paid out to victims who had a foreign government or international pressure groups behind them, it is not surprising that Roma and Sinti often found the German public and those officials responsible for making decisions on claims to be less than sympathetic.

Kurt May, a German of Jewish origin who led the United Restitution Organization's Frankfurt office was one of few to organize an appeal to the courts' denial of Romani and Sinti claims. In 1963, May and colleagues won an appeal and judges overturned a previous ruling, to accept that Nazi persecution of Gypsies on racial grounds had begun not only in 1943, but as early as 1938.

Individual Roma and Sinti filing claims for compensation often found their cases held up by numerous forms of bias. West Germany linked compensation to the "territorial principle", meaning that the applying victim had to have German nationality as well as meeting certain other criteria. Though most of the Romani and Sinti claimants did have German nationality, this was not always understood by the officials who reviewed claims.[84] A 1949 law resolved German citizenship, restoring it to those whose citizenship had been stripped by the Third Reich for religious, racial or political reasons, and to their descendants. This principle was, however, not consistently and fairly applied to Roma and Sinti. A circular distributed in 1952 by the Interior Minister of Lower Saxony advised: "Particular care must be taken in ascertaining the citizenship of Gypsies…" They were to be viewed with special suspicion.

Across many cases, one also sees that officials disregarded claims because of the prejudice that Gypsies are culturally or intrinsically nomadic. Those who fled Germany to other countries were often seen as following a migratory instinct, or *Wandertrieb* and so were denied classification as someone who had to flee or live in hiding from Nazi persecution. For example, Maria F.'s claim for compensation was rejected in 1961. She had escaped Germany in

1940, going to Slovakia and other countries before ending up in Italy. The claim was turned down based on the ill-informed belief of the reviewing official that there was no threat to Roma and Sinti in Germany in 1940 and that her flight from home was due, as the official wrote, to "the innately Gypsy migratory instinct". [85]

Some Roma wrote very pained, detailed and intimate letters of protest to high-ranking government leaders to ask their support with claims. Letters went to the President, the Chancellor, the President of the Lower House of Parliament and others.

Gerda S. wrote to Chancellor Willy Brandt's wife, Ruth in 1972. Her family had lived in a house before deportation. They were sedentary and always employed. In 1944 she and her three siblings had been given a choice between sterilization and a concentration camp and had, given the options, selected to be sterilized. They filed in 1947 for compensation and received nothing. She wrote: "The Third Reich robbed me of my health. It took from me the joy of being a mother. For over 20 years, I've suffered terribly from abdominal pain, but none of that counts…The Fourth Reich is throwing billions into compensation. Compensation for foreigners who suffered under the Nazis. I have nothing against that…but what I cannot understand is how there is no place for us…" Gerda related how she had found a husband who stuck by her despite her infertility. She asked help in receiving any small compensation that she could use to buy him a gift of appreciation. Her letter received no reply.

In 1971 the Central Committee of Sinti in West Germany was established. It took the Committee some time to find its footing but the organization quickly honed in on historical commemoration as a top priority.

At a Holocaust commemoration ceremony at the Bergen-Belsen concentration camp in 1979, attended by foreign and national dignitaries, Sinti and Roma victims were recognized as part of the event. Sinti community representatives came together with Jewish leaders, with members of parliament and the president of the European Parliament in perhaps the first public event with international attendance to give attention to the Gypsy genocide.

In 1980 twelve Sinti men held a fourteen-day hunger strike at the site of the Dachau concentration camp, demanding reparations and recognition. The event won the interest of the Social Democratic party, which took on discriminatory treatment of Sinti and Roma as a cause. The strike also led to agreement for the creation of a Sinti and Roma cultural center in Dachau.

In 1982, the West German government formally recognized the genocide of Roma and Sinti and the Central Committee was renamed the Central Council of German Sinti and Roma under the chairmanship of Romani Rose. The launch of the rebranded organization was marked by a visit from the head of state, Chancellor Helmut Schmidt. The organization's new name was, not by coincidence, similar to the name of the main Jewish community organization in West Germany. Soon there was a shift from claims made by inexperienced individuals to collective agency, with the Council filing claims on behalf of hundreds of especially needy persons.

Roma outside of the country, including a handful of American Roma were also at this time approaching the West German government about compensation. One John Ellis, owner of Ellis Motors, Inc. in Portland, Oregon and the self-proclaimed "King of the Gypsies of Oregon, Idaho, Wyoming and parts of Nevada" demanded that West Germany pay fifteen billion dollars to his authority "on behalf of all Gypsies throughout the world… for the annialation [sic] of over 400,000 of their people". This would not be the last attempt by people in America with no clear competence and no mandate from victims to seek monetary compensation for the Holocaust.

With even used car dealers in Portland, Oregon seeing that there was an opportunity for greater and perhaps more lucrative forms of official apology, Germany's Romani and Sinti communities were sorely in need of leadership and collective action. By the early 1980s, their population was larger than it had been before Nazism, not even including recently arrived "guest workers", or immigrant Roma from Eastern Europe. With these new arrivals taken into account, a study in West Germany in 1982 found that 25% of Roma and Sinti in the country were unemployed and 35% illiterate.

The creation of such a community institution did not bring overnight results. It certainly did not bring an immediate end to biases. In 1994 a survey for the American Jewish Committee found that 68% of questioned Germans did not want to live in a neighborhood with Gypsies. Many Roma, in this context, considered the Central Council and Romani Rose too focused on Holocaust compensation for Sinti. More generally, some felt that Rose's organization only addressed Sinti's concerns. Several Romani leaders arose to create new organizations in the late 1980s and early 1990s, to meet Romani community interests and especially to push for the needs of asylum seekers from the Balkans and Eastern Europe. While the new Romani organizations were intended to give attention to a wider range of issues, they too soon began to demand greater public awareness of the Romani and Sinti genocide and to complain about a common perception of history that leaves the Gypsies out.

Germany is not the only country where, despite an abrupt shift in power from fascists to those who opposed the old regime, the shift in attitudes toward Roma was far less dramatic. In Romania, for example, the Communist party that took power after the war chose an official version of history in which Romania had never gone along with Nazi extermination plans.[86] When the dictator Nicolae Ceaucescu fell and communism ended in 1989, the promotion of revisionist history only continued. Romani activists in Romania today struggle, as do others in much of Europe, to call attention to the havoc and crimes of the recent past.

Prejudices linger across Europe. In 1997, Jud Nirenberg visited Romani community leader Andrzej "Lulek" Wisniewski in Lodz, Poland, the same town where so many Roma and Jews died in the ghetto in the 1940s. Wisniewski was a soft-spoken and handsome man who wore carefully tailored suits at all times and had been a schoolteacher in Germany before returning to his hometown to establish a community center for Roma. He asked for international Romani cooperation in pressuring Polish police to arrest local skinhead youth who had attacked Roma. He showed Nirenberg and other visitors the swastikas and anti-Romani graffiti in the neighborhood near his office. "When Roma are poor," he protested, "they say 'We hate Gypsies because they don't work'. And when Roma are successful businesspeople, they say 'We hate them because they ostentatiously show off their wealth. They must be crooks.' We can't win."

Lulek Wisniewski (left) Rudko Kawczynski (center) and Jud Nirenberg (right), Budapest 1998

The Pew Center, a non-partisan research institution that conducts polls worldwide studied attitudes to minorities in several countries in 2009. Pew reported that 31% of Germans held negative views of Roma.[87] This is progress; 60% of West Germans and 57% of East Germans gave negative answers about Roma in 1989, meaning that prejudice was roughly halved in twenty years. The 2009 figures also make German attitudes enlightened by the standards of its neighborhood. 84% of Czechs expressed a dislike of Roma in 2009, as did 78% of Slovaks, 69% of Hungarians and 84% of Italians.

Some figures may be useful as benchmarks. 30% of Germans expressed unfavorable views of Turkish immigrants.

15% of Czechs, 29% of Hungarians, 27% of Slovaks and 29% of Poles had unfavorable views of Jews.

In the same project, Pew surveyed Americans on feelings about their minorities; 8% of Americans shared an unfavorable view of Black people. Even if one considers the United States to be an excellent model of race relations, Roma live in countries that have a long way to go before achieving such a model and face exponentially higher levels of bias.

In the view of many Roma and Sinti, education about the treatment of their people in the Holocaust is one part of the solution.

The Struggle for Holocaust Memory

Roma and Sinti across Europe mark each August 2nd as International Roma Holocaust Day. Since 2005, the European Roma and Travellers' Forum, which was for a time Europe's largest umbrella group of Romani organizations, holds an annual memorial event on the front steps of the Palace of Europe, where the Council of Europe meets in Strasbourg, France. The event is small but is attended by ambassadors and representatives of several European governments and usually by some French media.

The Polish government passed a resolution in 2011 to recognize the day, after years of hosting international gatherings on the date at the site of the Auschwitz-Birkenau camp. Hungary, Slovakia and Ukraine also now recognize the anniversary.

At last in April 2015, European Parliament formally made the date a European Roma Holocaust Memorial Day.

Romani *samudaripe* remembrances, memorial sites or exhibits can be found in several places across Europe, some of which have been noted. German Roma and Sinti have succeeded in having memorials erected in camps such as Ravensbruck and Buchenwald. Many more sites where Roma were slaughtered are left unobserved, both at the locations and in history books. Each memorial and each mention in history books is achieved with great effort.

From 1940 until the end of the war, Roma and Manouche were interned at the Montreuil-Bellay camp, run by France's Vichy regime (and for a few months by German soldiers). Over a thousand Gypsies were held there. After the camp was finally closed down it was quickly forgotten by historians and the public until Manouche schoolteacher and local historian Jacques Sigot published his own research on the camp in 1983. Its old barbed wire still surrounded the perimeter but was used to keep its more recent occupants, sheep inside.

With a friend and former prisoner named Jean-Louis Bauer, Sigot had a plaque made and placed on a stone put at the site in 1988. They and some friends paid out of their own pockets. It took two more years of letter writing, talking to journalists and to politicians before officials took interest. In 1990 President Mitterand intervened to make the site France's first, albeit small, Romani Holocaust memorial. Ever since, there has been a ceremony there every April in homage to Gypsy victims of World War Two.

The Montreuil-Bellay example reminds us of the background of all such memorials. Each tiny commemorative plaque, however easy to drive past without noticing and each event that gets even a couple sentences in just one local newspaper is the outcome of years of work by committed preservers of public memory.

The growth of the annual memorial service at Auschwitz-Birkenau is also not organic, nor the initiative of the managers of that museum site. It is thanks to a combination of hard work by, at the start, a single Romani activist and to the strange fortune that he happened to live in the town of Oscwiecim (the Polish name of Auschwitz). Roman Kwiatkowski formed his own non-profit association and worked for years to press the museum and government to support an event. A passionate, tenacious advocate of samudaripen commemoration, he did not always have it easy. He is a self-made entrepreneur. When Nirenberg first visited the Auschwitz museum in the early 1990s, Kwiatkowski welcomed him home for dinner. They ate Polish foods – a clear broth borscht, roasted chicken and traditional sides – but ate in a Romani manner, with knives and spoons but no forks, using the knife and fingers to eat. Nirenberg asked the unusually affluent Kwiatkowski what business had resulted in his material comfort and his ability to devote so much time to the volunteer pursuit of managing a charitable organization. Kwiatkowski was candid; gang activity. Nirenberg pushed for details. What did that mean, exactly? Real crime? Kwiatkowski shrugged. Mafia business, he said as plainly as if he were discussing a dry-cleaning shop. He had transitioned to full-time activist, living from savings and hiring a small staff to help expand the effort at Holocaust education.

For his past business dealings, Kwiatkowski was and still is treated personally as *marime*, or persona non grata by many Roma in Poland and abroad. He continues to pay for his past in the form of ostracism. Yet the association he built and leads cannot be slighted. Romani community leaders from across Europe and as far away as the U.S. and Australia come each year to take part in the event that would not have begun and grown without him.

When the European Roma and Travellers Forum approached the French *poste* about the creation of an August 2nd commemorative stamp, no funding was available. The Forum's board and staff contributed their own private money to arrange a small, online competition in which more than five thousand people across Europe voted on artists' designs. The selected stamp design by a non-Romani artist was used for a fifty Euro commemorative stamp printed in limited number. Twenty-five were sold. Robert Rustem, the Forum staffer who led the project laughs. "It's not about the number sold. What mattered was that it was a successful idea. More and more people got involved [in the voting]." Given the price, he was pleasantly surprised to sell so many.

The *poste* is now open, he says, to the prospect of re-launching the design on a normal stamp, to be made available at all French post offices.

At the time of this writing, Britain has a National Holocaust Commission. First set up under Prime Minister David Cameron, it still has had no Romani member. The twenty-six members include many Jewish and one Armenian community representative yet there is nobody to assure that the Romani community is informed of the Commission's work or that the Commission connects to Romani community resources, knowledge or concerns. Roma are often left out.

One commonly heard explanation for the lack of attention to the Romani and Sinti genocide is that the culture of the victims is to blame. While many have shown tenacity in seeking recognition of their peoples' losses, it is often remarked that Sinti and some Romani communities have strong taboos against even talking about the dead. For many Sinti and Manouche and some Roma, there are rules to avoid disturbing the spirits of the departed. For them, "the division between civilization and barbarism" says anthropologist Patrick

Williams, "is based upon respect for the dead". Manouche traditionally burned and still today generally do not keep the caravans or possessions of loved ones. Jewelry and valuables that cannot be burned may be sold to outsiders but the money's use is limited, usually allocated to the funeral and costs of the burial place. Among Sinti, Manouche and many Roma, one shares alcoholic drinks and even certain foods with ancestors by spilling some ritually to the ground but one does so without pronouncing a name.

Manouche will cease to say the name of a lost loved one for months or even years. Those who do say the name will always use it within a special construct that indicates appropriate respect. A man named Kalo may be mentioned, for example, always as "*u kuch Kalo*", or the departed Kalo. An alternate naming convention is often used. For example, a man named Kalo (which means Black) may always in death be referred to as "the un-white one".

None of this means, however, that Manouche, Sinti or Roma have an aversion to memorial ceremonies, sites or most other forms of official and collective respect for the dead. Manouche keep photos of the departed. They visit and maintain burial plots and tombstones. They often spend lavishly on their families' tombs.[88] The idea of a Romani or Sinti unwillingness to engage with Holocaust scholars, or a lack of interest in the development of historical commemoration sites and events is a myth, however convenient it may be to those who would prefer to imagine that Roma and Sinti do not mind being left out of the picture.

Historian Guenter Lewy has argued that Romani and Sinti victims of the Holocaust are not as known as the Jewish cases because of the highly publicized Nuremberg trials, which focused so much on Jewish survivors' testimonies. Not one Rom or Sinto was called to testify. Lewy may be inverting cause and effect. One should ask why not a single Gypsy was invited to testify. Lewy also notes that there were, in the years after the war, many Jewish survivors who wrote books about their experiences. It is from the writers that we know the Holocaust, whereas very few Roma or Sinti wrote their experiences. Again, however, the lack of Romani written testimonies can be seen as a symptom of the problem just as easily as its cause.

We ought to ask whether literary agents, publishers, ghostwriters and the reading public gave Romani survivor testimonies the same interest. We often imagine the author as one who writes simply because it is her calling, because she must get her story onto the page. In truth, encouragement and disinterest are important when a survivor is deciding whether to undertake the very difficult, time-consuming and perhaps re-traumatizing process of memoir writing.

When Romani American scholar Ian Hancock took the podium to talk at a Hillel Center, he says a woman stood up in the audience to yell at him. Why even talk about what happened to Gypsies in the 1940s as if it was in the same category as what was done to the Jews? Jews, she said, have given so much to the world and Roma were "parasites and thieves". The result of the lesser respect given to Roma and Sinti is an exclusion from memory. If this is not the *only* reason why Romani and Sinti deaths are left out of the story, it is one worth facing.

Museum curator Jud Newborn wanted to include Roma when preparing an exhibit at the Museum of Jewish Heritage in New York. He held an event for people from the Holocaust education field, including museum docents and teachers and found strong interest. "We had a good turn-out. All of them were more than sympathetic," he says. "No one in my own experience, as a Holocaust scholar or curator, has ever questioned the importance of telling the story of Europe's Roma in the Holocaust. I can't recall anyone ever protesting our inclusion of anything about the Roma community. The story in Washington [at the US Holocaust Memorial Museum], of course, was much different."

But as he continues to discuss his work, Newborn does recall prejudice. When he worked to include artifacts from Roma who had been deported from Romania in his museum's exhibition, he relates: "I was warned by one Holocaust scholar to regard the…artifacts with caution…that I might be scammed." Even when Holocaust survivors are donating family heirlooms to a museum, people assume that Roma must be working a con.

Whatever part biases may play, Roma and Sinti are often left out of the story. As Hancock notes, "the three and a half page entry for Romanies in the two volume, 2,000-page *Encyclopedia of the Holocaust*, incidentally, amounts to less than one quarter of one percent of the whole book, despite the enormity of Romani losses by 1945."

It is not only that the public or a few books have overlooked the Roma and Sinti. It is a norm among top names in Holocaust research and education. Hancock writes: "Professor [Yehuda] Bauer has been quoted as saying that Romani claims to the extent of their victimization in the Holocaust are 'all lies and fairy-tales' and that 'nothing happened to them' (Katz (K.), 1995); a statement which, if it were made publicly in Germany today about the Holocaust's Jewish victims, would result in a fine or a jail sentence. Indeed, as long ago as 1984, Yehuda Bauer dismissed Romanies from participating in the Holocaust." At a Holocaust conference in Stockholm in January 2000, Bauer told officials from the German government's Goethe Institute that certain representatives of the US Holocaust Memorial Museum were not invited specifically because "they belong to the last few examples of historians who still wrongly maintain that the Gypsies were victims of the Holocaust."

Hancock's memory tells us that the denial of Romani genocide in academia goes back at least as far as the mid-1980s. In fact, it goes back much further. In 1967 a symposium was held that included a panel discussion with Elie Wiesel, George Steiner and a few colleagues, none of them historians, called "Jewish Values in the Post-Holocaust Future". The word *unique* was used more than twenty times to describe the Jewish Holocaust. The participants were concerned that the Holocaust, as a symbol, would be taken away from its rightful owners. Wiesel noted that African American slums were called ghettoes and that the word Holocaust was used in discussions of Hiroshima. He said, "They're stealing the Holocaust from us."[89] Some important leaders in the Holocaust education sphere have long seen the Nazi persecution as property to be guarded.

History education always has an aim. African American history month in the U.S. is not only aimed at teaching history simply to enrich our knowledge of the past. It is meant to better our understanding of where that past has brought us, and of the current realities of a multi-ethnic society with problems remaining to be solved. Public education of the Jewish Holocaust is also not apolitical. It is often a part of efforts to achieve wider goals, including the confrontation of modern anti-Semitism or even, for some, to seek greater sympathy for Israel. In former Israeli ambassador Michael Oren's words, "Reasserting the factuality of the Holocaust is a pre-requisite for peace."[90]

Romani and Sinti human rights activists and community leaders today see Holocaust education and memory as important both because of our obligation to remember and honor the dead *and* as a component of a wider effort to confront modern prejudice. After all, the US Holocaust Memorial Museum's Krista Hegburg points out, the goal of Holocaust education cannot be merely to inform people that the genocide happened and that it was cruel. "When you see graffiti that says 'Gypsies to the gas' you have to see that the kids writing it *already know* there was a genocide." Holocaust awareness work is not intended only to give the facts of history but to shape how people feel about the past and, by extension, the present.

For the descendants of Rukeli, talking about his story is a starting point for classroom lessons about racism, offered by the family's non-profit association through local schools. Talking about the deportation of Roma and Sinti during the war can be a way, says Diana, to introduce the topic of Romani immigration to modern Germany. It is a sensitive issue. When her father gives talks about Rukeli's life and boxing, he always tries to tie it to the current matter of Roma seeking to immigrate to Germany from countries where discrimination is particularly strong. When politicians have been present at these talks, she says, "they just cut him off but we try to make people think". Deportation is not the only pressure point that connects current events to the Holocaust for Rukeli's family. Roma in countries such as Czechoslovakia were coerced to accept sterilization even into the 1980s. In recent years, as some women have continued to seek compensation in courts for racist health policies, the Trollmanns have been painfully reminded of Nazi sterilization efforts and convinced of the importance of talking about the fascist period.

British activist Grattan Puxon says, "You have to have a history to have a nation." For him, the Roma are a diaspora nation in need of a national awakening and symbols of unification. "We've had at least 200,000 Roma come into the UK in the last fifteen years and everyone has a story...a lot of survivors didn't want to talk about [the Holocaust]. Now the younger generation are working to revive the past. I wouldn't say we overemphasize the Holocaust. We put just as much energy into *other* days when we gather people to address our identity and past....we used to consider ourselves [the Romani people in the UK] a not very important Romani community in Europe and now the numbers *are* very important...and whenever there's a meeting the people are from all over Europe, from Bulgaria, Hungary, a unification going on in mini-scale." Holocaust, then, is shared history and an opportunity to offer people from varied countries a common historical reference. "So many of the people think only of what has happened in their own country [of origin], they'll say 'it's the Romanians [Romanian Roma] giving us other Roma a bad name'. We talk about the Holocaust and we talk about how it relates to what's happening now, how Roma are being deported now within the EU..." Like for the Trollmann family in Germany, Holocaust memory offers activists in the UK a natural segue into modern issues.

Sinto survivor Zoni Weisz was seven years old when his mother, father and siblings were arrested and murdered by the Nazis. He escaped because a policeman, seeing that he wanted to go with them, pulled him back and told him to disappear. He survived the war in hiding. He is today a member of the International Auschwitz Committee and has spoken about the Roma and Sinti Holocaust before the German Bundestag. For him, it is personal. "My family was murdered in the Holocaust. I'm the only survivor of my family. I'm convinced we have to talk about what happened seventy years ago, so that it will never happen again. Otherwise our loved ones have died for nothing. Without any reason." For him, the obligation to remember is a one-on-one, a personal connection to the deceased. "...we have a responsibility to tell our stories. In my opinion the suffering of each single person is much more important than the figures [statistics]. I'm trying to generate more publicity…because I think of my mother or my father or my sisters or my brother."[91]

Yet even for someone like Weisz, who leads in Holocaust memorial work in order to respect his own dead, there is a more practical and immediate political purpose. He sees Holocaust education as a warning or deterrent. "The world has learned nothing from the Holocaust" he worries. "Look around what happens now in the Middle East…I don't think it is going to happen in Western Europe again but we must look at the rise of right wing extremism throughout Europe. And let's not forget: Racism and exclusion of Sinti and Roma is still present."

Speaking with Romani and Sinti community organizers and activists who have struggled to have the Nazis' attempted genocide mentioned in Holocaust commemoration sites, events or publications, there is one issue that comes up again and again; Holocaust memory is turf and Roma do not have the strong organizations needed to fight for a piece of it. "Yad Vashem is a part of how Israel argues for its legitimacy. How do you include the Romani Holocaust in that narrative?" says Ethel Brooks.

"A large museum was built in Skopje [the capital of Macedonia] dedicated to the victims of World War II – the Jews, yet we did not even have an opportunity to participate in events marking the Holocaust in Skopje," says Asmet Elezovski, head of Macedonia's National Roma Center. For Elezovski, a Muslim like most Macedonian Roma, Holocaust memorial touches a nerve. Elezovski's grandfather was safe but many of his cousins, living in Italy and Austria, were deported to the camps in Poland. One relative survived and spent his last years of life in America. "I remember that in 1985 he came to visit and was quite old. He recounted the period with pain and sadness because he lost family. In the USA, he started a new family." Reconnecting was too difficult. The visitor, after one return to the land of his childhood, severed contact and focused on the present.

Elezovski believes that there was more attention to the Romani Holocaust in the past, when Macedonia was a part of Yugoslavia. "Access to education and curricula were quite different from today. At that time, there more public information about Roma victims during World War II, in Auschwitz, Jasenovac, Kragujevac. There were even movies dedicated to them."

One question, then, is whether political power is the issue , in which memory of the Holocaust a finite pie over which Roma lack the resources to compete.

Another question is how to frame events and how to talk about the Holocaust, which is not one story but the stories of millions. Nirenberg gave a talk on Romani community issues at New York University. A man in the audience stood to ask a question. We are drawn to stories of brave fighters in war, he said. We read about and remember heroes, soldiers. How can the Roma, who have never fought a war, make their history captivating and memorable? How can Romani history be of interest to non-Roma when it lacks bravery on the battlefield?

Putting aside the implication that heroism and bravery are only displayed through violence, the question was still predicated upon a very common but false notion. The Roma and Sinti have never had a nation-state and no war has ever been started by a Romani government, nor won by an army waving the Romani flag. Yet the idea that Roma and Sinti have only been victims in war is wrong. Franz Horvath, a Gypsy wrote a letter of protest in December 1938 to the Reich: "Many of our men were in the Great War and fought for the fatherland as well as any other. However, Dr. Portschy [Tobias Portschy, Area Commander of Styria and a contributor to Nazi race policy in regard to Gypsies] has not considered this. Dr. Portschy has taken away all our civil rights … I therefore see myself forced to lodge a complaint from us all at the highest offices of the government of the Reich." Horvath was correct in pointing out that many Roma and Sinti fought on the front lines. Moreover, Horvath was one of many who engaged in formal protest and advocacy, demanding respect for themselves, for their community and for basic principles. In a country where freedom of political expression or belief did not exist, was this kind of formal protest not a daring act of courage? People were sent to concentration camps for less.

To be a victim of majority oppression is *not* to be nothing else. One can be both victim and brave resistor. Rukeli was Nazi Germany's soldier as much as its victim. Roma and Sinti played many roles during the Second World War and many roles in effort to build less racist societies in the post-war period.

Why does Holocaust memory focus so much on the victimhood?

U.S.-based Romani writer Qristina Zavackova Cummings, whose grandfather served in the British military during the war after immigrating to the U.K. from Slovakia, says "in the history we read, or we hear, about the Holocaust there is very little pride…We're told Romanies were just rounded up and shipped off without a peep. That we were shot in our villages, massacred, burned…with not a word of protest…Meanwhile, we hear of the amazing resistance [of others] and the wonderful Jews who risked their lives to save other Jews."

Jan Yoors, the Belgian who lived with the Lowara and served in the Romani underground resistance, wrote *Crossing*, a memoir of his and his friends' bravery. Few other accounts of detail are left of Romani participation in the resistance. His son Kore comments: "With resistance work in any community, the less who knew what was going on the better." The number of survivors who have any knowledge to share, then, is limited. Further, he supposes, "Surviving all that trauma, there is the impulse to try to forget the past and move on…I think in Belgium, France…some resistance people who pushed for justice post war had political agendas/ambitions so [they] ended up shaping the discourse and communal memory… the Communist faction in France and, in Belgium, the Catholic or aristocratic stakeholders were controlling the dialogue." Roma and Sinti had no value in the narratives that were being constructed. Indeed, with rare exceptions such as a small memorial in Slovenia to Sinti who fought the Nazis, Sinti and Roma are rarely mentioned in commemoration of those who fought for Europe's freedom.

Finally, there is the complex question of where the story of the Romani *samudaripen*, or genocide belongs; is it to be told with the story of the Jewish Holocaust or given its own space, and what does each choice mean?

In 1988 a group of prominent Germans formed an initiative to propose a new (Jewish) Holocaust memorial in Berlin. By 1989, the group's leader, media personality Leah Rosh founded the civic movement Perspektiv Berlin and put out petitions "to finally build a visible memorial in Berlin to the millions of murdered Jews". While the official Jewish community initially announced that this was not a Jewish project and had nothing to do with them, Jewish leadership was quickly brought into negotiations on the future of the proposed site. Top intellectuals such as Gunter Grass and Willy Brandt signed on. Romani Rose, on behalf of the Central Council of German Sinti and Roma, quickly reacted with a full-page commentary in the daily *Tagesspiegel*. "The Holocaust also means the annihilation of 500,000 Sinti and Roma" he insisted. A memorial "that refers exclusively to the Jewish people implies a hierarchy of victims. This is hurtful and insulting to the victims of genocide and the survivors from the Sinti and Roma minority."

The issue was of special significance in a city that had only recently regained its position as the national capital and that was undergoing dramatic urban planning. Many worried that a row of war and genocide memorials in the center of the city would permanently reduce German history to its worst moments. Mayor of Berlin Eberhard Diepgen talked of *Denkmaleritis*, or memorialitis in a city that should become the "workshop of German unity".

Chancellor Kohl took a position in 1993, rejecting the call for a site that would remember both Jewish and Gypsy victims.

Romani Rose and the heads of the Jewish community - Heinz Galinski and later Ignatz Bubis - had a long, heated and often very public debate over the project.

In 1994, the main stakeholders – not including Rose and his organization - reached a compromise. There would be a central memorial just for Jewish victims. There would also be federal funds for a separate memorial to Sinti and Roma on land nearby, between the Brandenburg Gate and the Reichstag. The city would donate the land, 600 meters (2,000 feet) from the Jewish site.

Since the memorial was, among other things, a symbolic graveyard Bubis argued it was appropriate to treat it as a cemetery. The Jewish religion requires that a Jewish cemetery be kept separate from gentiles. 600 meters were determined to be an acceptable minimal distance between the Jewish (symbolic) graves and the Sinti and Romani site. Some common horticultural design, meaning the planting of the same trees, would give a sense of continuity between the memorials.

Rose again protested in newspaper ads. "Fifty years after the end of [Nazism], there is still no centrally located national Holocaust in the capital city of Berlin that commemorates the historically singular genocide of 500,000 Sinti and Roma and six million Jews. The Berlin Senate's resolution to erect a national Holocaust Memorial in memory of the murdered Jews of Europe…is unacceptable…the singularity of the Holocaust means that both memorials must be built concurrently on the same site…design of both memorials must guarantee that state gestures of national or international mourning and remembrance…for the murdered Sinti and Roma are conducted in the same way as they are for the murdered Jews."

The non-Gypsy, non-Jewish activists who had initiated the proposal were staunchly against the idea of a joint memorial. As their own newspaper ad argued, "Because every victim group has a distinct history, it would be disastrous to blend them together."

One leader of the group claimed, "If we are to include Sinti and Roma in this memorial, then we will have to also mention the Slavs and the mentally handicapped."[92]

Leah Rosh commented: "We would then also be expected to commemorate the German soldiers or the German housewife who was killed by bombs", as if Sinti who were killed in Auschwitz-

Birkenau for their race were no different than Germans who died while on the attack for Hitler's invasions.

In 1999 the issue of a "hierarchy of victims", as Rose called it, was still being debated in national parliament. The Bundestag president, Wolfgang Thierse, a Social Democrat opened the discussion with a speech in which he asked: "Do we want to dedicate this memorial to the murdered Jews of Europe or to all victims…murdered by the National Socialists?...We, as perpetrators have no right to arrogate a hierarchy of victims…we must ensure that our decision today does not in any way represent disrespect to the other victim groups – the Sinti and Roma, the politically persecuted, the homosexuals and the mentally handicapped." The session ended with a vote to expand the Holocaust Memorial so that it would include, in addition to Jews, a mention of "all of the other victims of the National Socialist crimes against humanity". The motion failed. The Bundestag then committed to funding construction of separate memorials in the city. There would be a site to remember Jews, another for Sinti and Roma and yet another eventually for homosexual victims.

It would take more than ten more years to go from this decision to the unveiling of a memorial to the Sinti and Roma. There were details over which to battle. For example, the Ministry of Culture wanted to call the site a memorial to *zigeuner*, or Gypsies. Romani Rose fought for it to be called a memorial to the Roma and Sinti.

Rose called Israeli artist Dani Karavan, whose work he had seen and whose unsuccessful proposal for the main, Jewish memorial site he had admired and asked if he could be commissioned to design the memorial. As a Jew, Rose told him, he might have more understanding of the Sinti and Romani sentiment about the memorial than other artists. Karavan, an energetic seventy year old was still smarting from the failed proposal, which had been "outside of their [the German selection committee's] imagination…I told him of course I would do it, though I didn't want to go through another long competition."

Karavan found the complications of working with dispassionate government officials and builders to be painful. "It put me in the hospital." He especially disliked the head of construction, who declined to include the Israeli artist in decisions about materials used. Karavan even engaged a lawyer to try to demand a change in the kinds of stones that were used. "He wanted a compromise but in art you can't make compromises of the heart. It's right or it's not." It is not only the artists who have such strong feelings about design decisions in Holocaust commemoration.

By the time the project was completed, Karavan was eighty-two. His work he says, had exposed him to four consecutive Ministers of Culture. "I said to the Germans: 'If it were for the Jews you'd have completed it long ago," says Karavan. "But because it's Gypsies, you're allowing yourselves to procrastinate.' For me as a Jew, it's easy to say this. The whole attitude here was one of scorn. Why spend money on this, what for? It's just for Gypsies."[93]

Karavan, whose grandmother and uncles perished in gas chambers, wishes there could have been one memorial for all victims. As he said at the memorial's inauguration, "I feel like my family was killed and burned with the Sinti and Roma in the same gas chambers and their ashes went with the wind to the fields. So we are together."

When the first stone was laid at the memorial Karavan attended and observed, along with the Minister of Culture and a group of survivors. It was Karavan's first encounter with Sinti and Roma survivors outside of Romani Rose's staff. He had attempted contact with others, such as the previously mentioned Zoni Weisz but had no replies. It was raining. An assistant to the Minister stood by his side with an umbrella. Elderly Sinti were left to soak. Karavan angrily noted the failure to see to their comfort. "If they had been Jews? You know?"

He sees Roma and Sinti as treated with less respect than Jews in modern Germany. "In a way the Jews are privileged because the Holocaust entered their culture after war." Here, he means that recognition of the Jewish Holocaust had impact on German culture. "So it was very important for me, as an Israeli Jew, to do this work for the Sinti and Roma as best as I could."[94]

The memorial is centered around a reflecting pool. In it, one can on most days see everything around the memorial; the German flag, the EU flag and the visitors looking into the waters. An unplanned effect of the reflection in the water is that a triangle shape on top of the Reichstag looks very much, Karavan feels, like the black triangle patch that Sinti and Roma wore in the camps.

While Rose's organization found the experience trying, the water in the pool may look half full to many Roma; Berlin does, after all the arguing, have a memorial site in a prime location, near other historic sites, recognizing the crimes of Nazism against the Sinti and Roma.

The story of the Berlin memorial demonstrates that respect for Holocaust victims is a sensitive issue in Germany, if at times a subject of contention. Perhaps because of the need to prove to oneself and to the world that the past has been confronted, Germany gives attention to the Gypsy genocide more willingly than some countries do.

For Rukeli's family, there were decades of quiet pain before some of the next generation chose to share their history. In the late 1980s, writers started coming to different family members and asking what people knew and could recount about the lost boxing champion. "The family noticed 'that a lot of people were benefitting from telling the story and it was not helping the Sinti community," says Diana. Some of the family thought it would be best to set up a non-profit that would control the rights to Johann Trollmann's name and memory and make sure that profits from media about him would be channeled into something to benefit young people. The association has printed a children's book about Rukeli that is used as part of classroom sessions about racism. The book is recommended by the Ministry of Education for lessons in the fourth and fifth grades. "We had a group come from Bremen - it's maybe three hours away - for the anti-racism talk, to learn about Rukeli," says Diana. "They loved it, I think." The group also sponsors sports and arts events at schools for Romani and Sinti young people and especially for refugees.

It was harder getting Rukeli's light-heavyweight champion title restored. "At first [the national boxing association] didn't want to do it but they agreed when there was public attention... after pressure from the media, they agreed to announce the title. We contacted the press agencies and German reporters and found interest from left-leaning newspapers. Some politicians from major parties were supportive. Greens especially."

Romani Rose was not responsive to the Trollmann family's letters at first. Once they had traction, however, he took notice. When they invited him to the event for the return of Rukeli's title, he attended. And when he learned of the children's book, he asked to be mentioned in an appended list of prominent Roma and Sinti. "We told him to go write a book about his own uncle and put his name in that," laughs Diana, who considered his openness to cooperation to be too little and too late.

Even at the press event where the belt was given to members of Rukeli's surviving family, Diana was disappointed that no representative of the boxing association came. "They said 'Even if we give it, it doesn't make him alive again'. And later they said 'OK, he's the champion now,' but they didn't want to produce the belt. That had to be done by a private supporter. In the end it was a small event in the backyard of a school, where they handed over the belt. If we had known, we would have refused to accept it that way. But another side of the family accepted it." She and the non-profit have more recently discussed the belt with the country's professional boxing association. She hopes to eventually hold a second event, "in a proper way" with more publicity, maybe even at the start of a title fight.

As noted, Tiefenthal Street, where Rukeli lived as a child was renamed Johann Trollmann Way in August 2004. This too required tenacious activism and some pragmatism. Initially, the family asked for the fighter's name to be given to a larger street. The selection of what is really a small alleyway with few addresses was a compromise. The family is not discouraged. "It's always a big struggle, a fight but we can make a lot of pressure, make people give a reason why not if they say no. Just no doesn't work anymore." The family hopes that in time they can convince municipal authorities in other cities where Rukeli fought to name streets for him and increase public awareness of both his life and of the Sinti losses in the Holocaust. Why not? "They have streets for Schmeling all over like that," reminds Diana.

Rukeli has been the subject of a biopic film in German, novels in both Germany and Italy and a play in Austria by the leading Austrian playwright Felix Mitterer. "We went to the play in Austria," Diana remembers. "Felix Mitterer contacted us with questions beforehand." He also made changes according to their notes. In an early draft, starving Sinti eat a horse. The family explained that most Sinti would sooner starve. "[Mitterer] invited us to the premier in Vienna. It was very nice…now we are in cooperation with a theater in Hannover and they are planning [to show it] also." Where Sinti victims are remembered, Rukeli is a common icon.

There may be a heightened concern and a lingering shame that makes the quest for Holocaust memory different in Germany. At the time of this writing, Rukeli's family have never had any contact with the US Holocaust Memorial Museum or with most of the larger Holocaust-focused institutions outside the German-speaking world. Well known (for a Sinto) in Germany and Austria, Trollmann is as absent, just as the Gypsy Holocaust is often absent, in worldwide Holocaust memory.

However and wherever one tells the stories of Roma and Sinti in the Holocaust, one might expect the US Holocaust Memorial Museum, a U.S. government institution in Washington, D.C. to stand out as an example of inclusion. It is a tremendous project aimed at delivering certain messages to the American and global public. It is intended, in its creators' words, to "help citizens of the world confront hatred, prevent genocide, promote human dignity, and strengthen democracy", using the Holocaust as an example of what must be prevented. The Museum, located across from the Washington Monument in the most prestigious spot on the National Mall was planned since 1979 and opened its doors in 1993 with a ceremony led by US President Clinton, Israeli President Herzog and other dignitaries. The first guest allowed through the doors to visit the exhibition was the Dalai Lama. A complex of red brick buildings, looking a bit like a concentration camp from the outside while also fitting the architectural style of other nearby federal museums, its current annual operating budget is $78 million, of which around $31 million is raised in private philanthropic contributions. It is the lead body in the American government's support, as well as a major receiver and spender of private funding to research and to telling the story of the Holocaust. One long-time employee quips, "You have to wonder what he'd think if Adolph could see the industry he created."

Yet, as Ian Hancock, a Romani scholar and former member of the Museum's Council (its governing board) puts it, "The U.S. Holocaust Memorial Museum has not yet done enough to educate the world about the Romani experience; there, the 'Gypsy' artifacts on display in the 'other victims' corner of the Museum's third floor consist of a violin, a wagon and a woman's dress--more Hollywood than Holocaust…despite the overwhelming amount of documentation relating to the fate of the Romanies in Nazi Germany which has been examined during the past fourteen years that the U.S. Holocaust Memorial Council has been in existence, that body, more than any other, rigorously persists in underestimating and under-representing that truth,""[95] Hancock's disappointment is mainly with the museum's leadership, noting that "staff, it should be said, have on the other hand generally been much more favorably disposed to the Romani case." He recalls when Professor Seymour Siegel, chairman at the time of the U.S. Holocaust Memorial Council "questioned, in the pages of the *Washington Post*, and in the context of their right to full inclusion, whether Romanies did in fact constitute a distinct ethnic people." Hitler, of course, thought so and that really is the point. Denying that Roma have been victims of ethnic persecution by denying that they are an ethnic group is like denying the existence of racism by saying "I don't see race." It is the perpetrator and not the bystander whose view of race is relevant.

Hancock is not alone in seeing the dominant American institution for Holocaust memorial as being negligent of Romani history.

Romani American documentary maker George Eli went there to film scenes for his documentary. Eli and his team were welcomed on a private tour. "The man who took us around was, maybe because he was in front of a Rom, very sympathetic and talked about how there should be more about Roma at the museum. I didn't feel like he was in a position to do anything about it but he was knowledgeable and sympathetic." Later, after a day and a half of filming, Eli found the Museum's management cold. "My opinion of the relationship is that the Museum is very passive. They don't want to start up anything. 'Yeah, yeah, Gypsies aren't included, we know.' But they won't do anything about it. I offered to show my film and they said they weren't showing films there anymore – which turned out not to be true."

Hancock will not forget when the Museum's acting executive director, Micah Naftalin told *The Washington Post* "The problem with Gypsies is that they're not well schooled. They're quite naïve…" These are the words from the head of an institution combatting ethnic intolerance. Where Eli sees laziness and bureaucracy, Hancock sees strong-willed refusal to acknowledge the genocide of Roma.

Ignorance may be partly to blame. Many people, even leading Holocaust historians, are simply unfamiliar with the facts of what happened. Just as some West German officials supposed that Sinti had left Nazi Germany because they are just habitual migrants, Roma today are often understood to be victims of the Nazis but of a lesser, very different category because of sheer ignorance. The old fallacy that Gypsies were punished as being migratory, homeless or unemployed comes up time and again in contradiction of the facts. Employed, home-owning Roma and Sinti with no criminal records were massacred and it was ultimately Nazi policy to wipe out the entire Romani and Sinti gene pool. Roma, like Jews, were guilty of being born and not of some bad action.

Hancock, in *Responses To The Porrajmos (The Romani Holocaust)*[96] gives examples of leading historians claiming that only Jews were marked by Nazism for complete extermination, whereas the plans for Roma and Sinti were only for nomads or came with lots of exemptions. In fact, the idea that sedentary Gypsies (those with long-term homes) should be spared was a recommendation but was rejected. While ostensibly nomadic Roma were arrested first, Nazi policy did not limit itself to killing the itinerant. As for other exemptions, clauses freed some Gypsies *and* some Jews from persecution in the beginning. By the end, the policy for both peoples developed into complete genocide.

Some historians also repeat the idea that only Jews were to be completely exterminated because there was a plan to keep a few "pure Gypsies" alive in special camps for anthropologists to study. Hancock clarifies:

"In the U.S. Holocaust Memorial Museum's published Holocaust history (Berenbaum, 1993:51) we find the same argument...that 'Pure gypsies were not targeted for extermination until 1942' (not true—but one might ask 'so what?'). The wording here gives the impression that there was an existing policy that was then revoked in 1942, rather than its having been...nothing more than a suggestion, by Himmler, which was mocked by his peers as 'one more of Himmler's hare-brained schemes'...and rejected outright by Bormann....Himmler might have wanted to create a zoo to display a limited number of selected 'pure' Gypsies, just as other Nazi leaders wanted to create museums to display Jewish artifacts, but...Himmler had to abandon his pet project (*Bundesarchiv Koblenz*, NS19/180)... even before this happened, 'pure' Sinti families in Hamburg and 'pure' Roma families in Vienna had been concentrated, registered, expropriated, and deported [to concentration camps]."

It has also been said that Roma were not victims of the same horrors as Jews because Germans liked Gypsies more than they liked Jews and treated them better in the concentration camps. Given the torture and ostensible medical experiments that the Romani prisoners suffered in the camps, this is an insensitive claim. The idea of preferential treatment often hinges on the decision at Auschwitz-Birkenau (and only at Auschwitz-Birkenau) to keep Gypsies together in family units, unlike other prisoners. This was not an act of kindness. The decision was made in order to avoid the bedlam caused by separating Romani adults and their children as they came out of the cattle cars at the camp. In the end, some transports of Jews to Auschwitz were also allowed by 1943 to stay together in families, the guards having learned from the experience with Roma and Sinti that it made people more manageable.

Hancock comments: "Some historians see only what they want to see, and...a very blind eye is being turned in the direction of Romani history, and that where the Romani genocide in Nazi Germany is acknowledged, it is kept, with a few notable exceptions...carefully separated...what does and does not qualify for inclusion in the Holocaust is a profoundly emotionally-charged issue, and one fraught with subjective interpretation and response. Assumptions are made, and repeated with confidence, by individuals who have no special expertise in Romani Holocaust history, and unqualified statements are reiterated which automatically assume a lesser status for Romanies in the ranking of human abuse."

It is not that Hancock sees nothing special about the Jewish Holocaust. He recognizes a distinction between civilians killed in war, however unjustly, even innocents killed for awful reasons such as their beliefs or private lives, and genocide, the effort of exterminating a race or nation in its entirety. It is simply that there were two ethnic groups and not one that the Germans marked for complete annihilation. He argues that Holocaust, with a capital H, refers to "implementation of the directive of the 'Final Solution,' *viz*. genocidal action intended to eradicate 'contaminants' from the Nordic gene pool in the creation of an intended master race. There were only two such directives: The Final Solution of the Jewish Question and The Final Solution of the Gypsy Question... Not one other group targeted in the Third Reich was slated for extermination, nor was the focus of a genocidal 'final solution.'" [97]

But what of his assertion that historians and the US Holocaust Memorial Museum are seeing "only what they want to see", and that the ignorance is at least partly willful?

Krista Hegburg is a staff member at the Museum. An anthropologist by education, she spent time researching Roma in Poland and the Czech Republic. She cautions against assumptions. Neither historians nor the public, and not even Romani activists know as much about the Romani genocide as we would expect, she says: "What we know about Jews and the Holocaust strikes us as natural and normative. 'This is what we know about the Jews so we must know this stuff about Roma'." Jews arrived post-Holocaust in the wealthier victor countries, such as the United States. Roma did not, at least not in the same numbers. Roma, for the most part, stayed behind and continued in important ways to suffer persecution after the war. No ethnic or national project helped the Romani refugees to build a new home. "We expect people to know – at least Roma and experts – about the Holocaust and the Romani experience because people know what happened to the Jews. But there are a unique set of conditions that produced the big museums, the scholarship…it's an unrealistic expectation even for the activists to know."

In other words, a greater ignorance is to be expected in the case of the Romani genocide. Yet Hegburg does not deny that there is a conflict or that some of the Museum's founders and current overseers wish to maintain the Holocaust as distinctly Jewish turf. The Museum, she says, is "a product of the Jewish community" and more specifically of a predominantly German and Ashkenazic Jewish community with priorities that even some other Jewish groups might find exclusive. It is an institution created to teach the history of European anti-Semitism.

There are side exhibits at the Museum to teach visitors – the Museum has greeted 30 million people to date – about genocides around the world and contemporary discrimination issues. The Museum is very open to holding temporary exhibits about the Khmer genocide in Cambodia, about Darfur, etc.

It is less open to educating the public about the oppression of Roma. Is an exhibit about genocide in Africa less threatening than mention of the Roma, whose genocide in Europe is a part of The Holocaust? Are Roma different because the request is not for a slice of pie at the Museum but for a slice of the same pie? "Oh, absolutely," says Hegburg. Her own work has generally focused on engaging with other (that is, non-Jewish) minority groups. "One of the reasons they hired me was to take information out of the Museum to colleges, disperse them out into the world and do what I'd call minority inclusion." The Museum has shown interest, often implemented by Hegburg, in outreach to historically Black colleges and in building forms of cooperation with scholars in African-American studies, Latino studies and other fields. The Museum does wish to reach or benefit people with an interest in connecting the genocide of the Jews in Europe to other cases of ethnic persecution in history or today. Something just makes the integration of the Romani story into Holocaust memory especially tricky.

The push to have Roma and Sinti included in the Museum's public education began almost as soon as the planning for the Museum, years before its inauguration. Activist Grattan Puxon lived from 1982 to 1985 in Los Angeles and had the chance to take part in some of the earliest efforts. He had used savings to move from the U.K. and set up a small news agency that covered the fishing industry and other specialized topics, as well as doing some other odd jobs at times. Puxon joined up with a small core group of Roma across the United States who would go together to Washington, D.C. and lobby for some sort of Romani participation in planning of the eventual Museum. The group was mostly made up of men from one community, the Vlax Roma whose culturally conservative tribes had come from the 1880s through the early twentieth century to America. They were unschooled but entrepreneurial men from all over the US. John Marino from Los Angeles, John Tene from the Boston area and Jimmy Marks from Washington state were part of the team. Ronald Lee came from Canada. Marks presented himself as the most affluent and offered himself as the ringleader. "He wasn't interested in the Museum per se but [New York-based Romani activist] George Kaslov reached out to him," says relative and filmmaker George Eli, quoted previously. "He was trying to get the Museum to include Roma. And Jimmy was wealthy for a Rom and had a good head on his shoulders." Eli grants that Marks was eccentric and a "fame addict" but also reminds that he was a generous one. "If people needed a few thousand dollars to keep the [Holocaust advocacy] going, Jimmy would help them."

Puxon remembers Marks at a Holocaust commemoration event at which the idea of the Museum was furthered. "He was an audacious person. There were maybe fifteen of us standing outside the Capitol and some of us were in prisoner costumes." John Tene and other Roma from Boston had rented the concentration camp props. "When George Bush went up to the podium to speak, Jimmy walked right up behind him and took a seat up there."

Tene had filled a van with Roma and driven down from Boston, and arranged for everyone to stay at a Ramada Inn. Someone, Puxon tries to remember who, referred to the plan to get Roma onto whatever board or committee would run the Museum as a "cockamamie scheme". He cannot come up with the name.

It was a leader on the Council to create the museum, Seymour Siegel and he was speaking on record to the Washington Post.

If the idea was cockamamie, it was not hopeless. Simon Wiesenthal wrote to the Council to support the Roma's position. As retold by Hancock, "Simon Wiesenthal's book *Justice Not Vengeance*... expresses his dismay at the Council's attitude towards Romanies..."

"On this council sat voting representatives not only of the Jews but of Poles, Russians and Ukrainians—but not Roma. Efforts in that connection by the International Romani Union were in vain. To help them, I wrote a lengthy letter to Elie Wiesel the president of the Council. A few months later I received an answer from his secretary that the appointment of members depended on President Reagan. The International Romani Union and The Society for Threatened Peoples thereupon wrote long letters to President Reagan—which ended up with Elie Wiesel."

They banged on all possible doors to ask for attention to their idea. "The *Washington Times* covered our meeting and there was a picture," Puxon tells. "The paper said it was a picture of a concentration camp survivor. He'd never been out of the US...We booked a room in the basement of the hotel and did a commemoration there...I think we had a good echo when Romani Rose came over."

Were the main creators of the Museum open to working with the Roma? "Not at all. Totally cockamamie. They had a whole idea of 'Gypsies', they didn't know a damned thing about them...and there was a lot of quarrelling about the facts." The Roma and the historians they met fought over how many Roma might have died under Nazism. "And there's a lot more documentation now." Puxon says there is much more material and documentation now thanks to

Romani Rose and others. "The numbers of Roma who died has changed as the information has been brought together."

The Roma at the Ramada in Washington, D.C. did not include John Ellis of Oregon. He was, however, active on the question of how the Museum would deal with Roma. In 1984, the same year of the meeting, he hired a lawyer to approach Republican Senator Mark Hatfield (who had fought in the Pacific in World War II) and to ask help in assuring that the Council in charge of the Museum would include a representative of the Romani people. The attorney, Frederic Cornilles could neither correctly spell Holocaust in his correspondence on the issue nor make clear why his client, the "King of the Gypsies" and auto dealer Ellis would be an appropriate choice to govern the Museum. His work did not brand the Romani agenda well among the Museum's creators. He did, however, make the straightforward points that Roma were victims of the Nazis, that Hatfield had Romani constituents and that representation of Roma somehow on the Council was important to them.

Puxon thought the best chance for a Romani person on the Council was Marino. But there was soon a more likely, more educated candidate. Ian Hancock, the English-born Romani who taught linguistics at the University of Texas seemed more the type that would fit. The Council was not meant to be a committee of historians or academics; its members, appointed by the President of the United States, were to be politically connected. They would be the sort of people to give or get large donations for the Museum. Still, Hancock was a published expert on Roma as well as a community member. Given that there was no one among the small set of activists who fit the same profile as the Jewish Council members, a scholar seemed like as good a fit as could be found.

Bill Duna, a Romani American and college music instructor living in Minnesota remembers getting to know Hancock. Hancock wanted to speak Romani, to test whether Duna was truly a Rom. "I thought he was joking," says Duna.

Duna's family came from Hungary and Slovakia and had been musicians and blacksmiths for as far back as he knows. They came in the late 1800s to Pittsburgh and to Cleveland because these were places with large Central European immigrant populations who wanted to hear Romani music. Duna's great grandfather was a musician and booking agent. His father won a scholarship to Juliard but did not go. A cellist, he became a professional musician without the advantages of that sort of education. Bill Duna too grew up to make a career of music.

Duna's uncles fought in the war, some in Europe and others in the Pacific. European relatives died in the camps. But growing up, he did not even know that Roma were victims of the Holocaust. "You'd go see a movie and there'd be newsreels showing the concentration camps. They showed the ovens. And one time they said 'this is where they burned the Jews, Gypsies and many others'. And I thought 'Gypsies?' We didn't know this until the war was over. People never talked about the Roma."

He came to the issue of Romani Holocaust memory indirectly. Before that, his fight was for something that he felt affected his own household more directly. "When I was a young kid, I was maybe in my thirties, one of my kids came home with *'Where the Sidewalk Ends'* written by what's his name, the Jewish writer [Shel Silverstein]. And there's a poem, *The Gypsies Are Coming*, about how the Gypsies take children away. It's a poem for children, telling them how bad we are as a people. Holy smoke, here's a guy who's Jewish, years after the Holocaust and he's doing this. If you said this today about Black people, about Jews - but here it is. And my son was sad. He was upset. Everyone at schools knows we're Gypsies and the kids in class all made fun of him. That was the beginning of me becoming an activist." Duna tracked down Silverstein to talk with him directly. In the days before the Internet he learned that his public library, for a fee, could come up with the writer's home number. Duna told him how the story had upset his son and Silverstein took offense. "Why don't you change it to The Jews Are Coming?" That would be racist, said Silverstein. "That's right, you son of a bitch', and I hung up on him." He enlisted a lawyer, who was his friend and piano student. The son and the lawyer wrote Silverstein's publisher and sued. The publisher, after months of arguing, folded. In editions now, the poem is reformed as *The Goonies are Coming*.

Having learned that one can fight for some respect for Roma and win, Duna wanted to become more proactive in shaping how people see his ethnicity. He began to look for the books that would give a more appropriate image of his people.

He came across a book about American Roma. He picked it up with great interest and hope, then read it in anger. The group of Roma that the writer, an anthropologist had chosen to present as representative of all Romani culture was from a community that makes a living from fortune-telling, confidence jobs and fraud. They were criminals. The book presented this as not the way of life in one small group of Roma but rather as the Romani American culture. Duna called the writer, Ann Sutherland, who happened to also live and teach, like Duna, in Minnesota. He told her off.

She had focused on nomadic people and ignored Roma like Duna's family, who had lived in and owned houses for centuries. They met and he showed her old family photos. "The people in your book are chicken thieves. That's not who *we* are. You make it out like you're an expert and all Roma are thieves just because you found someone who lives that way." She assured him that when she next wrote about Roma, she would make clear that all Roma are not the same. And it was she who introduced him to Ian Hancock, who drew him into the circle of activists trying to get Hancock onto the Council for the future museum.

Duna went with Hancock and some of the other Roma to a meeting with members of the museum's early Council, including chairperson Elie Wiesel. The Council was making an effort to at least meet with Roma and to discuss how to include the Roma and Sinti in the story that the museum would tell. And the Roma were still using the most aggressive means they could think of to demand the Council's continued attention. Some activists – in Duna's memory they were not Roma at all but locally recruited college students – wore concentration camp costumes and marched in front of the meeting.

Inside, the conflict was not only between the Council and the Romani community representatives. There was also distrust between the Roma.

Duna says, "You know these fortune-teller Rom, there's always a big chief. Meeting with the Museum was a status thing for them. Our family is not like that." When he was growing up, Duna's family told him to stay away from the fortune telling families that lived in their town. Now he found himself with the very kind of people he had always heard about. They were uneducated, they made a living in cash on the gray market and they raised eyebrows even as they tried to convince non-Roma to take their cause more seriously. "The [Vlax] Roma thought they could get money out of the Holocaust to start a school for their people, but they weren't organized enough to push the Museum to help with anything."

Duna's apprehension toward his fellow activists was not the only fissure. He says Romani Rose, who so rarely came out of Germany to work with Roma, was distrustful of Ian Hancock.

Despite the challenges, the Council was feeling the pressure to include Roma in some way and opened up to the possibility of a Romani member of the Council. Hancock, however, was not eligible. Born in England, he was not a US citizen. The small team discussed their options.

"None of them on the Council wanted any Roma but there were some articles in the papers, we were getting some publicity so they really had to. They wanted a token," says Duna. And with Hancock ineligible, "Ian needed a puppet... I was always talking with him. I always called him after Council meetings to keep him filled in. He would have been great for the Council but couldn't get in."

Duna was, like Hancock, in higher education. When not working as a college music teacher, he taught music clinics around the country and had written a book for children on music. Like Hancock, therefore, one could deacribe him as published. With Hancock out, Duna became the replacement candidate. He met Congressman Tom Lantos, a friend of the Museum and of the Romani cause. Lantos, a

Jewish Hungarian Holocaust survivor and California Democrat helped to push for Duna to join the Council and later cooperated with Duna in looking into how to make restitution easier for Romani Holocaust victims and their families. "When I met him, I met his wife, Annette and I said 'You look just like Zsa Zsa Gabor.' She said, 'that's my cousin.' We got along. She loved Gypsy music and we connected. She and her husband were real movers and shakers in Washington." After the Congressman's passing, the Lantos Foundation for Human Rights and Justice was formed. The Foundation continues to take interest in contemporary discrimination against Roma in Europe and sponsors one Romani student each semester from Europe to serve an internship with a US Member of the House or Senate. Some of these students have gone on to take important community leadership roles in their own countries and to work for equality.

Duna, with the Congressman's support, was finally asked formally if he was interested in serving on the Council. In Hancock's understanding, Duna would serve until Hancock could become a citizen.[98] "I said 'If you can't find anybody else, I'll think about it'," sighs Duna. He joined in 1987. Hancock sums up, "It took seven years after its creation for the sixty-five member Holocaust Council to appoint even one Romani representative."

He ended up serving two terms, staying through the creation of the Museum until 1997 and even seeking a seat on the Council's executive committee, though this was not approved. In his role, he came to know Sybil Milton, the head historian for the Museum who had a strong interest in Roma and, according to some colleagues, in the story of Trollmann, who so far remained undiscovered by the public in Germany and beyond. Other key staff at the Museum such as Michael Berenbaum were cynical about Roma in Duna's estimation. "Michael Berenbaum wrote that Jews were the only group singled out as a race. He wouldn't say that Gypsies were also singled out. He'd just delete them. He would leave things out."

Even with a Romani person on the Council and even with a few key allies, the Roma found that the planning of the Museum and its activities did not incorporate Roma and Sinti. Duna sat in the hot seat. Roma called him in the middle of the night. "You're not a real Rom, our people are real," he remembers them telling him. They pressed him for help getting Holocaust compensation funds – not for victims but for the Romani community in general – from the Museum somehow, as though the Museum were planned to become an all purpose grant-making institution. At events he organized about the Romani genocide, Romani elders came up and told him they wanted to take the podium and speak. He found himself in the unpleasant position of explaining the program was fixed and that there was no open microphone component of the event. Some argued that they were important leaders. They could not imagine how he was allowed to speak and they were not. "You're not *my* king, I had to tell them."

The Museum began to organize an annual event called the Days of Remembrance, which would bring together members of Congress and the Senate, Holocaust survivors, the media and others. Duna wanted Roma at the ceremony. He successfully pushed for a seat on the organizing committee for the Days but then for two years could not convince his fellow committee members to involve Roma in any way.

And then Elie Wiesel, who had long argued that the word Holocaust could never refer to Roma and Sinti, resigned as chairperson of the Council. There was an opening, a crack in the wall. Duna threatened to bring Roma to hold a protest on the street if Roma were not included in the upcoming Days. With a letter of support from Simon Wiesenthal for the Romani cause, the post-Wiesel Council finally caved in.

The event was held at the Capitol Rotunda, the US Capitol's landmark dome. A Romani musician came and played violin and a Romani woman joined honored Jewish guests in lighting menorah candles.

Duna also set up a separate event for Roma in Chicago, where he had relatives and knew a sizeable community. The Chicago candle lighting for the Roma received local press coverage. "I planned that whole thing. I wanted to do the same thing in Washington but there was all that resistance to it. We could have had someone come and play music, we could have filled the venue. They didn't want it."

The next year, he tried to change the format of the Days of Remembrance. It had seemed in the past year as if the Romani woman was simply paying homage to the Jewish dead by joining in a menorah lighting. He suggested that the event could have all the candles to represent the six million Jews and a single rose to represent the Roma. The idea was accepted. Duna's great nephew, nine years old, would go up to the podium with the rose. He calculated that the child would stand out among the elderly Jewish representatives who lit candles. "And that's how we started to get included in the Days of Remembrance." In fact, it is both how representation of Roma started and ended at the Days of Remembrance. In later years, there was no inclusion in the program, though a few Roma have been in the audience.

More important to him than the ceremony was the development of a Children's Exhibit. In 1988 Duna wrote to other Council members, copying the New York Times and other media, to complain that Roma were not included in the planned exhibit. Isaiah Kuperstein, Director of Education for the museum told him that fate of Romani children could not be mentioned in the exhibit because, Duna quotes, "Gypsies didn't have a normal home life". He disputed this, reminding that Roma were mostly *not* nomadic before (or after) war. "This was not true. You have to remember the villages that existed before and after the war…they were doing medical experiments on Romani children and none of these kids are shown [in the exhibit]."

A private donor contributed two million for the exhibit. Duna believes the donor was given a voice in the discussion and wanted it only for Jewish children. "Do you know how many Gypsy children died in the Holocaust? It was at least hundreds of thousands and nobody knows even today because so many were killed right there where the Nazis found them. But the exhibit wasn't for them." To this day, he regrets that the exhibit still tours the country no reference to Roma.

Years after leaving the Council, he took his family to see the exhibit when it traveled to Chicago. There was still not even a mention of Roma. He called the Museum and finished the conversation believing that he was promised a change. "The people who make the decisions are not the people who work at the Museum, it's the big pockets. And they don't want Roma."

Duna was successful in getting the Museum to make some information available to visitors with an interest. With Sybil Milton's help, pamphlets about Roma and other non-Jewish groups were given out for free – they were not displayed but were handed out to visitors who walked up to Museum staff and enquired. In time, Milton and Duna convinced the Museum's bookstore to keep one book on Roma. After years of activist complaints on the issue, there are now sometimes as many as four books about Roma in stock. Regretfully, this seems to be the most enduring legacy of Duna's years of energy and determination.

Some people at the Museum who interacted with Duna have remarked that they found him over his head, neither as informed about the Holocaust nor as politically savvy as other Council members. One staffer saw him give a talk at a film festival in New York. "He tearfully told the audience that white people stole *flamingo* from the Gypsies. Flamingo. And he was the music expert."

A Romani American tells of seeing him speak at a conference in Texas. "He was weeping during his presentation, he really had his heart in it. But also he did not have a lot of detailed information about the Holocaust or the Museum's plans."

He is a passionate advocate of the memory of the Romani dead if his familiarity with the Holocaust is not always that of a scholar. Commenting on the difficulty of winning compensation for Romani victims, he says: "Roosevelt created a group to look at what to do about Israel and in that group were the Rothchilds. Look them up. They were Jewish and they were very wealthy. Anyway, deals were made. At Nuremberg, there were about twelve prosecutors of Jewish descent. They had an agreement that they wanted to bring out in public what happened to the Jews in the Holocaust…look at the transcripts and you'll see the Nazis saying 'yes, we did these things to Jews and we did them to Gypsies' but that wasn't what the people in charge wanted to focus on. The trials were largely about the creation of the state of Israel....They downplayed Roma."

"I met [Nuremberg trials prosecutor] Ben Ferencz when I was a speaker about Roma at a gathering of surviving Nuremberg prosecutors. This is over twenty years ago...I asked him why no Roma got anything, why they weren't reparated [*sic*]. And he said 'It's simple, they had no political power.'" Duna remembers Ferencz working the room in a double breasted suit, with one hand tucked into it. "Like Napoleon. A little guy with a lot of power walking around with his hand in there, just like Napoleon."

Council members were never meant to be experts on the Holocaust. Their role was and is governance of a large institution, not academic substance. The Museum employs some of the world's top authorities on the history. Council members are, however, mostly erudite and politically well heeled. Duna got by on personal charm and is rich in terms of people skills. It was, unfortunately, not enough for what he or the Roma aimed to achieve with the Museum.

He needed to do more than be graceful. He needed to swim upstream and to erase the memory of those involved in the Museum whose views of Roma had already been tainted by the likes of John Ellis, and those who saw Holocaust memory as a potential cash source for arguably worthy projects such as vocational school for young Roma. Hancock acknowledges, "I had a couple of friends who wanted to claim reparations as survivors, but their families actually arrived here in 1921." Any Romani voice on the Council had to work against the perception that Roma had an opportunistic approach.

Duna looks back on his ten years of participation in the Council and his continued advocacy as having gained little ground. "I got up and spoke at the [Council] meetings but nobody listened. Nothing changed. Ian [Hancock] should have been on the Council from the beginning. He used to give me a lot of documentation to give to the museum, about Roma in the Holocaust."

"You go up to the third floor of the Museum and you find a [Romani] wagon and they have a couple photos of kids. They look handicapped, maybe with mental disabilities. That's the image they give of the Roma. Nomads and damaged minds… And there are some other pictures of Gypsy children on display, except they don't say they're Romani children." Roma can be invisible in the Museum even when their photos are chosen for display. In the Museum as in so many places, Roma are often only noticed at all when fitting a stereotype.

Duna is not alone in taking offense at the lone spot in the Museum that mentions the Roma, presenting a wagon, violin and colorful Carmen-style skirt. Over decades of complaint, the Museum has neither increased the amount of content about Roma on display nor replaced images that Roma have described as stereotypical and hurtful.

As for Hancock, he soon had his own turn on the Council, from 1998-2002.

Hancock was raised in London, with family roots among the English Romanitchals as well as Hungarian Roma. A linguist who teaches at the University of Texas, he is a leading authority, though an advocate of controversial theories, on Creole languages in Africa and North America. He was the first scholar to do field work on Texas' Afro-Seminole Creole.

Like others interviewed, he sees Holocaust commemoration as an essential piece in a more complex puzzle. "I teach Holocaust as a genocide, a program of mass ethnic cleansing in order to create a 'master race', which is why Jews and Roma have to be classified together. When I teach genocide as a topic, I use…proposed breakdowns of the 'steps' or early warning signs in a society that foreshadow an impending possible genocide. It starts with bullying, then progresses to demeaning a people (such as in cartoons, jokes) then unchallenged police targeting, then legislation, then incarceration, sterilization and so on. I use the Littell steps, but there are a couple of others. We see some of these steps out there now."

And like some other Roma interviewed, he feels regret at having grown up with so little education or awareness about the Holocaust. "In London...my Uncle Albert, who maintained ties between England and relatives in Hungary, told me that some of my distant relatives were listed for incarceration by the Nazis." He laments knowing so little about them and their fate. "I didn't even know about it as a kid, so there was no discussion. The War, of course, was a constant topic. We didn't know what was happening to Romanies or Jews...When I got to this country I certainly heard a lot about the Holocaust, but only about its Jewish victims. Roma here had vague ideas about the Romani victims, but most American Roma came to America long before the Holocaust happened... I learnt about it as I got older, but the turning point really, for me, was when I learnt that the USHMMC [the Council] had not appointed a Romani member."

When he joined in 1998, he was determined to open the eyes of the Holocaust research and education community to the facts of the Romani genocide. He aimed to convince their leading thinkers of the need to include Roma and Sinti in the story. While he was more knowledgeable than Duna about the Holocaust and, as a long-time employee of a large state university, perhaps also more prepared to deal with the Museum's hierarchies and bureaucracies, Hancock's accomplishments did not exceed his predecessor's.

One employee of the Museum says cautiously, "I have an excellent relationship with Ian but it's a sophisticated one."

"During my four years as a Council member, I was invisible." Hancock later wrote. "William Duna would call me after each of his own visits to Washington, always shaken and hurt. 'I thought I was a decent person' he told me once, 'but I come back from these meetings feeling completely degraded.' On one occasion, at a January 1991 meeting of the U.S. Holocaust Memorial Council's Annual Days of Remembrance planning committee, when asked by Bill Duna when Romanies would ever be included as well, chairman Benjamin Meed replied 'Ask me again in about twenty years.'"

"My own experience matched Duna's—members were for the most part distant; some were even openly hostile. ...Eleven Clinton appointees were replaced by the Bush administration, but no new Romanies were selected to fill any seats."

Can the conflicts Duna or Hancock had with the Museum be all written off as the Roma's fault, as a lack of diplomacy or understanding?

On some level, a degree of inherent tension is to be expected between the wishes of Romani activists – on or off the Council - and of the historians who are the institution's workforce regarding the public message that the Museum presents. There are different perspectives and priorities.

One historian at the Museum says: "I'm not very comfortable with some Roma activists because they give no support [to historians' work] but when they feel there is not enough attention to their group, they come and complain…some of these activists are very loud, very aggressive. I know wonderful Roma activists but I don't like superficial activism." If there is an anti-Roma bias in this remark, it is that it leaves the impression that the Romani community is somehow different from the Jewish organized community in seeing Holocaust education as a means to an end. In fact, Jewish activists also interact with the Museum and also have aims that go beyond the purely academic; there are goals such as the combatting of contemporary anti-Semitism and, for some, the support of Zionism.

Acknowledging that some give and take between activists - whether they are on the Council or not - and Museum staff is part of the game, Hancock ruffled feathers and not only of those who wore an anti-Gypsy prejudice on their sleeves. A Museum program manager calls him "a 1970s-style ethnic studies scholar-activist who wedges open a space for activists, to make claims for community representation. That kind of person doesn't step back and let younger people [with other skill sets or knowledge] talk when the time comes." To be the kind of person that Hancock had to be, in order to win those first gains of recognition in the 1970s and 1980s, is to have the kind of aggressive personality that maneuvers less successfully once the doors to cooperation are opened.

Looking back at the 1998-2002 period, Ethel Brooks says, "I don't think we [Romani activists] achieved anything. There were programs, conferences, there is some recognition of the issue because of Ian's work. He shook things up. He was unruly-" she begins, stops. "Is part of the lesson that the grand narrative can't be changed?" In other words, can we care about the Jewish persecution and even respect its centrality in the Holocaust narrative, and still give more attention to the Roma?

Why have all Romani requests for more visibility in the exhibit(s) of the Museum been unsuccessful? And why can the one small display about Roma not be replaced with something that Roma themselves do not describe as stereotypical and offensive?

Petra Gelbart, a Czech-born Romani woman who first became interested in the Romani genocide while a student at Harvard University, has been active in pressing the Museum and other institutions in the United States, including the UN in New York to give Roma more voice and presence in Holocaust commemoration. For her, the bottom line - money - is the bottom line. "There are no Roma who are major donors...I wish that didn't matter. I wish people at the Museum would just do the right thing and involve Roma in decision about the images that represent real Roma in the exhibit, instead of having a wagon and a skirt."

Another Romani scholar with a long history of interaction at the Museum refuses to go on record but agrees that there is an anti-Romani agenda among the (fund contributing) Council members. Current opposition at the Museum, she asserts, "is at the highest levels. It's not the staff. And that's why there's so much material in the archives."

In Brook's view, the staff's open mindedness leads to a great deal of excellent research and documentation.

What, then, keeps material from appearing as part of the public messaging, the exhibits?

For Radu Ioanid, a historian and author working at the Museum who is eager to see more work on the Roma – "they died with us and they are a part of the history," he says - the difficulty has nothing to do with donors or the Council. "The Council has nothing to do with the permanent exhibition…Changes to the exhibition are slow."

It has been decades. Can change that slow really not be a sign that someone in charge is actively against the change? He shrugs. "It's not the Council."

In the view of Krista Hegburg too, the problem is not rooted in a deliberate opposition to the wishes of the Romani community. The Museum supports and enables a wealth of research of Roma and Sinti that just never leads to additions or changes in the content of the tourist experience, the exhibits of the Museum. "A lot of the centers within the Museum are walled off from the permanent exhibit. There are silos everywhere [in big organizations] but the USHMM is particularly silo-ized." Maybe Duna and Hancock just never really communicated with the right people, she wonders.

Hegburg does more generally blame the Museum itself for the failure to work well with Romani community advocates, including Duna and Hancock. "Sometimes people at the Museum screwed things up with the Roma, not that they weren't trying but they were too casual about the issue, didn't see how important it was and the screw-ups over time become systemic…the run-ins with Bill that make a community feel excluded…not necessarily hard to fix and they don't get fixed over ten years. There's an inability to hear what Roma are saying. And it's one thing if you exclude one person one time but here's a people, Eastern European Roma, for whom most of life is exclusion and we reproduce it. You can say 'OK, we didn't invite you to that one conference.' But these are conditions that control people's lives as secondary citizens in Eastern Europe and leaving them off the invitation list just, you know…"

She recalls incidents that would be detrimental to even the thicker-skinned Romani activist. "Things have come up where the response [of the Council] has been, 'well, we don't do actually do that…and we do, but they didn't care."

It is disappointing to someone who, like Hegburg, has lived in and knows countries where the Holocaust happened. She believes that the Museum should pay close attention to modern anti-Romani discrimination, especially as the Museum aims to be a source of information and analysis on present day ethnic discrimination and its potential for escalation. "When you see the anti-Semitism manifest itself in obvious ways in Hungary today, the people [using hate speech] are also anti-Roma...people who focus on the anti-Semitism don't pay attention to Roma as the canary in the coal mine."

Whatever the failings or victories of the two Romani men who sat on the Museum's Council then, there is a place for greater attention to Roma and Sinti in Holocaust studies and the US Holocaust Memorial Museum. Since 2002, when Hancock's term ended, the Museum has had no Romani participation in its leadership or staff and no positive change in how it teaches the history of the Romani and Sinti *samudaripe*.

Starting in 2011, the name of one Romani American scholar, Ethel Brooks became a refrain, advocated by Roma to become a Council member. For years, the push to win her a seat on the Council continued with support from friends in government but without a decisive response from the Museum.

Brooks is a professor of sociology and gender studies at Rutgers. She grew up in a close-knit Romanitchel (English Gypsy) community in New England. Her family traces back for five generations in America, part of the family having come from Britain in the 1830s and others later. They were among the first settlers of the Gypsy Hill neighborhood in the greater Fall River area of Massachusetts, and her aunts and uncles still lived there when she was little. In the 1970s, the city of Somerset took the family's land on Gypsy Hill by eminent domain. In the Brooks family when Ethel was growing up, all the men joined the Freemasons and everyone spoke Anglo-Romani, the *poggardi chib* or *broken tongue* of English Romanies.

Her father and uncles fought in the Second World War. Coming from military service to live in a solidly Republican community in

New Hampshire, her father was passionately anti-war. Her mother formed close friendships with a circle of Jewish women and for a time even brought Ethel to synagogue, where she first heard about the Holocaust. As a small child, she heard the shocking story of Jewish skin used by Nazis for lampshades produced in the camps. She was vaguely aware that Roma were also targeted for genocide, but only as a young adult did she relate the Holocaust to her own Romani identity or consider it as a focus of her work.

"When you begin to look at Romani history, you can't avoid it although, to be honest, when I was in college or even graduate school I didn't plan to work on the Holocaust. I just – I thought it would be too difficult. I had worked on questions of solidarity work with people in Nicaragua and post-war countries' questions were central to my work. I was interested in *that* but wasn't going to look at the Holocaust. And I didn't want to do Romani-themed scholarship. I had tried to do my graduate thesis on Roma in the interwar period and on their economic productivity ...but when I presented that at Gypsy Lore Society meetings [The Society is an international forum for anthropologists and other academics studying Roma.], I found those old time Gypsy Lorists were nasty and dismissive and wanted to know how I dared to question the canon of the Gypsy Lore Society. I felt that part of why the history of Roma was ignored by wider historical scholarship was the continuing legacy of that Society, into the '90s. I was a twenty-something scholar and went back to my advisor...My advisor warned me to stay away from that minefield and so I decided to stay away from Romani topics in general. I stayed on my other work, though it was always in the back of my head...Eventually, as a scholar of Romani descent, you can't avoid the Holocaust and I still just didn't know how to connect it."

As a professor at Rutgers, she was invited to an event that reintroduced the subject matter to her. "A colleague had invited me to be a respondent at a conference on sociological responses to the Holocaust. We were reading papers about testimonies and people's letters, and it was all about Jewish survivorhood...it must have been around 2003, and my comments all revolved around what happens when we add Romani and Sinti history to the mix." The comments went into a book called *Sociology Confronts the Holocaust*, published by

Duke University Press. "A few years after that, Rutgers got access to the USC Shoah Foundation Visual History Archive, founded by Steven Spielberg" she recalls, referring to the film producer's charitable foundation that collected testimonies of survivors on video. While the foundation began by focusing on Jewish survivors, it in time included Roma from some countries. "We had a new dean, Doug Greenberg. He had been CEO of the Shoah Foundation before coming to Rutgers and asked everyone, 'What are you interested in?'." Brooks told him she was interested in Romani studies. "And he said 'Do I have something for you!'" Rutgers was going to be one of few American universities with full access to the Spielberg archive, with over 400 Romani testimonies.

She started to look at the oral histories, "hiding in my office for weeks on end and being blown away". That was the moment when she saw the possibilities in Holocaust studies and the opportunity cost of leaving the work to someone else, who might never come along. She wishes there were a multimedia journal that could fully use the testimonies she examined but she has written a paper on Romani women's testimonies and how they disrupt the usual story.

"What shifts when we listen carefully to Romani testimonies and in particular Romani women's testimonies? For years, I gave scholarly papers but getting into activism – I remember meeting you [Nirenberg] and I spoke with Ian [Hancock] in maybe 1989 - but I have to say that I didn't expect to be a kind of activist or to become prominent in the field. I just started to give papers on the Holocaust. I'm not sure when I met [other Romani activists in America] but I thought, 'They're doing amazing work and I'm in academics.'" She makes academics sound dirty. "I'm not sure how it happened that this is now my work."

For a long time, she felt that she could only stay in academia and did not imagine herself in work that would make her an *activist*. Activism meant standing up and speaking both on behalf of, and to Roma.

"It was so gendered. I felt like I was on the outside and couldn't ever be a leader in that way...I was so conditioned to seeing men as the movers and shakers that I didn't consider what I could do [on

Romani issues]...My first interaction with the Museum was when Krista Hegburg suggested that I look at what the Museum was doing on Romani history. She didn't work there at the time. But because of her, I applied for a fellowship. It might have been 2010. You go for a seminar for five days."

Hegburg does not completely agree with this version. In her memory, Brooks had already been identified by Erika Schlager, senior counsel at the US Commission on Security and Cooperation in Europe as a good candidate for a future Romani member of the Council. Hegburg does remember discussing the fellowship and the Museum. (The Commission, made of both US Members of the House and Senate, guides much of US policy-making in regard to Roma and Sinti in Europe.)

Brooks presented a paper on Holocaust testimonies in Austin, organized by Ian Hancock in 2010, using her learning from the fellowship. Hancock and Duna were there. She did not feel herself being drafted into any collective effort. "Maybe someone saw me as a cute young *Romni* [Romani woman] to charm but that's it."

In 2011, she had another fellowship, this time at the USC Shoah Foundation and at last started to take Holocaust scholarship seriously as a focal point of Romani activism. Even then, she says that she did not yet see any potential for Roma to work with the Museum. Erika Schlager asked her then if she would be interested in being on the Council. "And I said if I can help yes, of course but then again I said that I didn't see what I could do. Bill had been on the Council and then Ian and, you know, what had that done?" The letter from Capitol Hill to the Museum about Brooks in 2011 did not go very far. "Ian knew about that. I contacted him and asked what he thought. He said 'It's probably not going to happen.'"

Four years after first being formally proposed to the Council, Brooks is still waiting for the invitation to join. In the meanwhile, there is no ongoing Romani movement pushing for Romani inclusion at the Museum, though Roma continue to resent that they are not more present as speakers at events, as subjects of side exhibits, or otherwise. Sympathetic people in official positions, such as Erika

Schlager make an effort to bring Roma into the picture without much steady impetus from Romani community organizations.

Why would it take five years to get from *"maybe"* to *"maybe"* with Brooks' nomination to the Council? "This is where Romani-Americans come in," she says, noting that the lack of consistent and well planned advocacy by an organized community is necessary for some changes. "Romani-American letters of endorsement have helped. Since when we [Brooks, Nirenberg and other Romani Americans] went to Washington in 2013, there was a bit more pressure. And Erika...learned how to move this forward." She elaborates that Schlager and the US Commission for Security and Cooperation in Europe have begun to encourage Romani American campaigning. "But I think it's about the Washington focus of the Romani American activist community." A Romani person on the Council of the Museum may give Roma some voice. But the Romani community usually lacks the strong voice needed to achieve goals such as getting a Romani person once more onto the Council.

Professor Brooks is convinced of the importance for Roma and Sinti to continue to push for public awareness of the *samudaripen*. "The Holocaust is a big part of US public, collective memory. But how do we talk about Romani and Sinti history as a part of that story? We've been left out of it. Even as the survivors die off, the second and third generation care about this part of history and talking about the Romani and Sinti part of the story is important to recognition as survivors."

Like others, she relates the importance to combatting current extremism in Europe. "Holocaust denial is illegal in many countries but...Romani Holocaust denial is still acceptable. It is common for people to deny our Holocaust....there are so many genocides that are either forgotten or not quite forgotten but faced with a lack of recognition that survivors and their families deserve. And also there's now the whole idea that the trauma of genocide is, in ways, passed down through generations... Without the recognition that should be granted, you can't deal in any way on the community level with it... [Telling the story of the Romani genocide] brings us into world history...and there is a global solidarity that comes from survivordom."

And while the discussion of the US Holocaust Memorial Museum can leave us with the sense of stagnation, awareness has been won elsewhere, in Europe.

"When this year the European Parliament recognized August Second, that was a huge milestone," Brooks reminds. "Poland was already using the date but now it's different, it's on the European level and that's key." There are other successes. "Look at Romani Rose's work. It has been key in Europe, culminating with the Heidelberg Center and the memorial in Berlin. And look at the gatherings on August Second in Auschwitz and Krakow [and now, on a smaller scale, in other cities around Europe]. That's a third milestone. We need to celebrate that and build on it. The work done to mark May 16th and the Romani uprising in Auschwitz also creates opportunity for much more recognition."

"And the work that you [Nirenberg] and I and Petra [Gelbart] and other US-based activists have done with the UN." The UN Secretariat in New York hosts an annual Holocaust commemoration with diplomats from around the world. While Roma were included in the program in 2011 and 2013, the UN office in charge of the event usually refuses to include Roma.

"I know it's been frustrating but I think we've made progress. There is a recognition that every so often they have to bring in a Romani speaker. I think we're almost at a tipping point where Roma aren't just lumped into 'other victims'. I do remember when Yehuda Bauer stood up [in 2014] in London at a meeting with the International Holocaust Remembrance Alliance and said that the Jewish deaths were the only Holocaust. And Roma were there to stand up and speak back. We're frustrated, yes and now the survivor generation is dying and compensation might not happen. That's a tragedy. But other points of recognition are possible and, I think, important."

One the very day when this book's writing was completed, the White House announced is appointment of Brooks to the US Holocaust Memorial Museum Council.

Rukeli's fight and that of the Roma and Sinti for an equal place in society is neither over nor futile. As the work goes on, Rukeli continues, as an example to a few, to give hope and inspiration.

Ethel Brooks at UN Holocaust memorial ceremony in New York

Where the Genocide is Remembered

A review of the ways that the Romani genocide has been ignored can give the impression that nobody does teach the *samudaripen*. Yet in 2003 all countries of Europe and the former Soviet Union, as well as the United States and Canada signed the Organization for Security and Cooperation in Europe (OSCE) Action Plan for Improving the Situation of Roma and Sinti. This agreement contains a commitment to "include Roma history and culture in educational texts, with particular consideration given to the experience of Roma and Sinti people during the Holocaust". The agreement was developed by OSCE Senior Advisor on Roma and Sinti Issues Nicolae Gheorghe with the assistance of Jud Nirenberg, who was charged with assuring that Romani civil society inputs were collected and used in the text of the agreement. Today, the agreement is in one way or another put into practice by roughly half the countries that signed it. The OSCE continues to monitor and report on participating countries' implementation of the Action Plan. A few countries where the preceding story takes place, and how they teach or fail to teach history, are mentioned below.

In Austria, the Ministry of Education arranges for Roma and Sinti to visit schools and give talks about the genocide. On May 5th, the country observes the liberation of the Mauthausen concentration camp. Romani victims are included in the ceremony. Leaders of the Romani and Sinti community also participate along with politicians and others at an annual event at a memorial site in the place of the Lackenbach detention camp, in Burgenland.

In Belgium, the Kazerne Dossin Museum, which receives many school field trips, has information about Roma as part of its permanent museum. Students who do not happen to have field trips to this museum are likely to learn nothing about the genocide of Roma and Sinti, or anything else about Roma in European history.

Bulgaria is, along with Romania, one of the two countries in the world with the largest Romani communities. Teaching about the Romani genocide is not, according to the Bulgarian government, currently offered in primary schools, high schools or universities. There is also no teacher training available on the subject.

In the Czech Republic, activists continue to pressure the government to build a fitting museum or memorial site at the location of the Lety concentration camp, where there is now a plaque on a rock in the woods where the camp stood. Much of the former camp site is used today by a pork farm. European Parliament has formally urged the Czech government to buy out and shut down the pig farm and to put a more informative and suitable memorial on the location, to no result.

Still, non-profits including Brno's Museum of Romani Culture gather each year on August 2nd at the site, joined by Czech and foreign officials. The Museum and other organizations also hold a memorial event annually at Hodonin's former Gypsy Camp, to mark the occasion of August 21, 1943 when the camp's prisoners were sent to Auschwitz.

The Czech Ministry of Education shares links to online information about the Romani genocide to make the material accessible to teachers.

In France, the government supports no special commemorative event. It has, however, officially recognized the genocide and over the years, as previously noted, a French President and representatives of the Foreign Ministry have attended various Romani genocide memorial occasions.

The states of Germany have autonomy in deciding much educational curricula but some Holocaust education is mandatory in all of Germany. Seven of twenty-six German states now teach the Romani and Sinti genocide. Roma are not only referenced in Holocaust education; other states include education about Roma in other history lessons or in classes about human rights and other themes. Teachers' guides are made available about the *samudaripen* and students go on field trips to concentration camps in Germany, as well as to camps such as Ravensbruck in neighboring Austria.

In the Baltic countries of Lithuania and Latvia, where more than half of Roma perished, there are also teachers' training materials. Since 2009, the Lithuanian Ministry of Culture has worked with Romani community leaders to hold a ceremony at the Paneriai Holocaust Memorial Center in Vilnius, bringing together Members of Parliament with Roma and representatives of the Jewish community.

Macedonia, whose Holocaust memorials are mentioned in a preceding chapter, has one of the largest Romani communities in Europe as a percentage of national population. Macedonia has not replied to the OSCE's questionnaire about how or whether the Romani genocide is taught.

Poland has reported to the OSCE that "teachers decide how the subject of national and ethnic minorities is taught, while taking into consideration the needs and competences of their students." The Polish government has reported that there are no official teaching materials about the Roma and Sinti genocide. Still, as previously discussed, the government-supported museum at Auschwitz provides information about Romani genocide to its visitors and holds an annual memorial on August 2nd. Some Romani non-profits have also received government support for small public education programs.

In Romania, the Ministry of Education has training courses for teachers, in partnership with UNICEF and the Romani charity Romani CRISS, about Romani culture and history. In 2006, the Ministry put out a calendar of activities and events that teachers may choose as opportunities to teach about Roma and the genocide.

There are not, however, any references to Romani history – neither Romania's history of slavery nor the Holocaust – in the history books that are normally distributed to students in Romania. The available materials and lessons are only used by teachers who seek them out and, on their own initiative, prepare lessons for their classes.

In Slovakia, Romani non-profits began cooperating with the Ministry of Culture in 2005 with the aim of creating engraved stones or plaques at sites relevant to the *samudaripen*. Today there are commemorative objects across the country, in the previously mentioned village of Lutila and in Banska Bystrica, Nemecka (where mass executions took place), Hanusovce nad Toplou, Zvolen Slatina and Dubnica nad Vahom.

Slovenia, whose Sinti community is referenced early in the book, responded to the OSCE questionnaire with a *non sequitor*, sharing no information about Holocaust education but instead noting an EU-funded project to hire Roma as teachers' assistants.

Spain is another of the countries with the largest Gypsy populations. Until present, the Spanish government has begun no concrete activities to teach the public or even teachers about the Romani genocide.

Ukraine also reports no effort to teach educators or students but does support scholarly research into the topic.

The United States did not reply to the OSCE questions about how the Romani genocide is taught within the United States. The United States is, however, vocal on the subject of Romani genocide memory, using diplomacy to remind European partner governments of their own commitments. Congress encouraged the White House to appoint a Romani person to the Council of the US Holocaust Memorial Museum.

Race Politics in Sport Today: Andrea Pirlo and Tyson Fury

Andrea Pirlo is one of Italy's and Europe's top soccer stars. He has played for his country's national team, for New York's professional club and for Milan and has won the FIFA World Cup. *The Guardian* ranked him among the world's top ten players in 2012. For years, Italian media remarked on Pirlo's supposed Sinto heritage and at times addressed his career decisions and his mobility from team to team as indicators of his "Gypsy" character.

In his 2013 autobiography, *Penso Quindi Gioco (I think, therefore I play.)*, he responds to the rumors. He is *not* Sinto.

"At first I left it alone,"[99] he writes. "Then the media bombardment became untenable. In addition to the production of wine, my father is involved in the steel industry. Since trade and recycling of metals are traditionally widespread among Sinti, someone wanted to make [him] into one…if I had denied it in a strong manner, I would have risked offending someone…distancing myself from a community…a risk I did not want to run for the simple reason that racists make me sick. I am not Sinti but to say it publicly could have created a series of errors…"

It is a sign of progress – or at least worth commending Pirlo – that his wish to avoid feeding anti-Sinti bias was stronger than the urge to clarify his own ethnic roots. (He identifies himself as Lombard.) If Pirlo is an indicator of any trend, maybe the story shows a change for the better. Yet it also shows that sports stars who rise and fall on their own efforts are still treated by the media and the public as somehow emblems of ethnic groups. Their successes and failures are still seen as proving something about those of us who are merely sitting and watching from the stands. In the case of the Sinti and the Roma, society has not stopped its rush to mix real athletes' efforts with imaginary ideas. Sports commentaries still expose myth and prejudice regarding Gypsies.

In the world of boxing, Tyson Fury took the world heavyweight title from Wladimir Klitschko in Dusseldorf, Germany in November 2015.

Fury puts his ethnic identity at the center of his story. "I'm glad I'm Romani. My Traveller origins have given me determination and the will to win, to keep going until I touch rock bottom. There is no defeatism in me."

While the British Fury, from an Irish Traveller family, has received enthusiastic social media support from Irish boxing fans, he makes his loyalties clear. "I'm not Irish or English. I'm a Gypsy." And boxing is as much a part of his family culture as his ethnicity. His family tree includes the legendary bareknuckle fighting champion Bartley Gorman. His father, another champion bareknuckle boxer, named him after Mike Tyson. Fury's team includes his uncle and trainer, Peter and his cousin and sparring partner, Hughie (who has represented Britain in amateur competition).

Fury, despite his family's successes in the ring, was raised in hard conditions. According to a 2014 *Guardian* study, Travellers have the highest infant mortality of any ethnic group in Britain and have a life expectancy twelve years shorter than the national average. Fury was one of only four children to survive of his mother's fourteen pregnancies. He is quick to speak of the poverty and marginalization that Romani and Traveller people continue to face in Britain. "We may be the same colour, and we may speak the same language," he says of the Irish Travellers, but "…we are aliens."

Fury says that prejudice remains in today's sports fandom. "I get it every day," he says. "'You gypsy bastard, you fat gyppo.' All sorts of stuff. It's mainly the Facebook warriors." Hate speech against Gypsies is ndeed especially common on social media. *Wired* magazine noted in 2016 that the top two most used hate speech terms used in Tweets from the UK are anti-Gypsy slang words.[100]

Fellow Traveller and boxer Billy Joe Saunders has similarly pointed out that pejoratives like "gyppo" and "pikey" have not disappeared in the age of multiculturalism but have instead become increasingly common.

In the British professional media, however, the attention tends to respectfully keep distance from references to his ethnicity. His roots cannot be completely ignored, nor perhaps should they be, as he chooses to mention them, calling himself the "Gypsy King". Still, the focus on his ethnicity in British press is mainly in reaction to his own focus upon it. Things have changed since the days of Johann "Gibsy" Trollmann.

For Fury to identify as Romani is also an indicator of a shift. Members of the Irish Traveller community are often quick to point out the difference between their heritage and that of the Roma. There is, in fact, no link between the two groups other than both being called "Gypsies". Fury's use of the word Romani to describe himself is the sort of cultural amalgamation or dissolution that Romani Rose and other Sinti leaders have sought to avoid ever since founding their own organizations. As barriers come down and European (and worldwide) "Gypsy" communities have more opportunity to learn about one another, the Romani identity dominates and spreads. This is both a sign that the Romani identity is a growing source of pride, at least for some, and a sign that Romani culture and identity can pose a challenge to smaller so-called "Gypsy" ethnicities like Irish Travellers or the Sinti.

At the end of 2015, Fury was a candidate for the BBC Sports Personality of the Year.

His own views on the matter oscillated. "Hopefully I don't win," he tweeted, "as I'm not the best role model in the world."

A few days later, he was insulted at the many protests against his nomination coming from a public responding to allegations that he had made sexist and homophobic remarks in interviews. Among other controversial statements, the Born Again Christian told an interviewer: "There are only three things that need to be accomplished before the devil comes home: one of them is homosexuality being legal in countries, one of them is abortion and the other one's paedophilia."

He called BBC radio to defend himself. "I believe I should be winning Sports Personality of the Year because if it's about sporting achievement, and personality, then I'm a winner hands down."

So shortly after stating that he did not want to win, he said on Twitter that his critics "can suck my balls" and pledged to continue to be a "roll model *[sic]*".

Even while many Roma were celebrating his achievement, others were wincing. As Bill Bila, organizer of a Romani LGBTQ group warily put it, "He is a world champion and…we want to be proud. We *want* him to be an example."

Fury, then, is no Trollmann, Schmeling or Pirlo in terms of his social consciousness. Nonetheless, he exhibits a deep concern for his community and a sense of social responsibility. In between offensive tweets and interviews, he trains for a fundraising exhibition for his home city Manchester's children's hospital and participates in church life.

In the end, he was not selected for the BBC honor but was chosen to be *Ring* boxing magazine's 2015 Athlete of the Year.

Fury's success shows that today's Europe offers chances and interethnic respect that Johann Trollmann's did not. A proud and outspoken Romani or Traveller can be a national and world champion.

His success also shows that minorities who hear so much about an increasingly multicultural and tolerant Europe but so rarely see the proof – the Irish Travellers, the Roma and other groups regarded suspiciously as Gypsies – continue to produce some of the world's bravest fighters, in and out of the ring.

Bokhale Mulenca / With Hungry Ghosts
By Qristina Cummings

As Bibi and I stood together at the side of the road, she self-consciously picked at the sleeve of her sweater. I knew that bruise-blue numbers crawled there, marking her as *subhuman*. We never talked about it and she always tried to keep them covered, but sometimes when we were cooking she'd roll up her sleeves and I'd see them there, glaring and crooked. In the crackling silence of night, she'd sit in front of the fire, whiskey in one hand, pipe in the other and repeat the names of her lost relatives.

Dinah, František, Alina, Asja, Leszek, Ješenja, Duša, Albina, Tomasz, Rozali...
each one heavier than the last.

Scholar Jeffrey C. Alexander (2004) claims that "cultural trauma occurs when members of a collective feel they have been subjected to a horrendous event that leaves an indelible mark upon their group consciousness, marking their memory forever and changing their future identity in fundamental and irrevocable ways". Alexander also pointed out that, in order for an event to be represented as cultural trauma, *the event must be culturally classified by the collective as a master narrative, one which constructs the core of its collective identity*. Smelser (2004) also suggests that, in order for an event to be considered a cultural trauma, the memory of the event must be culturally and publicly represented as obliterating, damaging, and as a threat, both to the existence of the culture with which the individual identifies and to one's own identity and self.

For Maami and her surviving family, their future identities were certainly shaped in "fundamental and irrevocable ways". They fled their homes, they lost two-thirds of their siblings, parents, cousins, aunts, and uncles. They lost their livelihoods. They were haunted forever by the hungry smoke and its terror. Whether this was felt by the whole *collective* as a *master narrative* is somewhat debatable. Maami, Papu, and others focused on a positive and useful sense of historical events - not on the truth of them. For example, many stories that referenced anything related to the War were told as cautionary tales, as reference manuals for how to deal with being *illegal* and *unwanted*. Many stories featured the hungry smoke - wisps of cold that crawled in the night, suffocating and stealing entire families, leaving nothing behind. There was no *master narrative* - no "story producing all other stories". Their memories were coloured with the green and gold of sunlit forests, the black-brown of newly turned earth, and yes - the pale, creeping metaphor of *hungry smoke* - but this smoke was not the entirety of their memories.

The traumas they suffered were like pebbles - hundreds of smooth, round, grey pebbles - stacking wearily on top of one another. This one a beating by the *Hlinkova Garda;* this one a week without food; this one a squalling baby gone silent and bloated in the night; this one and this one the *SS Einsatzgruppen;* all of them adding to the weight of their lives. Some were jagged - memories of loved ones faces, torn in terror; Dachau; Dysentery - cracking the smooth facade of *life after*.

E mašina maj piskinel,
Chore Romen maj ladinen.
Chore Roma avka roven,
bo len l'idzhan pre šibena.

E mašina maj piskinel,
Chore Romen maj ladinen.
Roven, roven, chore Roma
sar len l'idzhan pre šibena.

Romale, Romale, ma roven
de, imar pale na avena.
Jaj, de mamo so kerava,
imar amen murdarena.

On the other hand, Papo and Baba Edita, they lived in relative safety. The blitz and its bombs visible on the horizon through the corners of torn blackout paper, sometimes the ground shaking from their impact, but all in all *safe*. The *Holocaust* a word they had no understanding of. They heard of relatives passing, but always simply shrugged, puffed their cigarette and said, "people die in wars". Their narratives held different, slower rhythms: The clip-clop of

Hmara's hooves as they were asked to move on again; the gentle sound of rain on the hedgerows; shouts of "dirty black pigs" echoing through the still air. They *fled*, but there was less urgency, less immediacy.

Narratives from both sides of my family were viewed through a unique filter - the idea of the past reappearing in the present, the melding of two different times as indistinguishable from each other. Experiences of *before the War* and *after the War* are very different for Baba Edita and Maami Babka, yet each expressed them in the same way - a colliding of today with yesterday and of tomorrow with now. Nostalgia was a way of forgetting, of surviving, of bringing together the disparate narratives of a *diaspora*. Over all, the stories had the same roots, the same shadows and lights, though some were more suffocating than others. Eyerman (2004) argues that, "as opposed to psychological or physical trauma which involves a wound and the experience of great emotional anguish by an individual, cultural trauma refers to a dramatic loss of identity and meaning, a tear in the social fabric, affecting a group of people who have achieved some degree of cohesion. In this sense, the trauma need not necessarily be felt by everyone in a group or have been directly experienced by any or all."

The meta-narrative has shaped Romani lives all over the world. Whether or not my relatives directly experienced the horrors of the Holocaust, our histories are bloated and stinking with other, hideous half-hidden truths - slavery, branding, rape and forced assimilation, mutilation, hanging, beating and humiliation, sterilization, murder... each torment cracking holes in our stories, creating a descent into "wordless nothing" (Arthur Frank, 1995) in the face of such traumatic and chaotic memories. However, Mikhail Bakhtin (1981, 1984) emphasizes the social perspective of language, that language is spoken (and written) between and among language users: it is a dialogic interaction, a process whereby communities of speakers are always co-creating the meaning of the language they utter to each other.

In this regard, the silences in the oral histories my grandparents told spoke as loudly as all the words combined. The words they simply couldn't bring themselves to speak clattered conspicuously at our feet. Words like *rape, execution, murder, concentration camp*. The hungry smoke devoured everything, including the words it defined. It left hungry ghosts in its wake - those unable to rest, those seeking their families. It left terror and silence.

Our lives were forever affected by its presence - the poverty, alcoholism, and silence tore its way through our families. Stories were corralled behind whisky bottles and Maami's skirts. I absorbed the words and their absences. My childhood was cradled in the soft breath of horses as we rocked our way through life. But, there was always a sense of something coming, something *terrible*. We didn't trust, we didn't settle, we didn't integrate. We waited. Our history shimmered distantly, sometimes brought into sharp focus by the crooked, crawling bruise-coloured tattoo on Bibi's arm, or the tears Maami could no longer suppress for her lost relatives. The Post-Traumatic Stress that caused my grandmother's hands to shake and reach for the bottle crawled its way into my father and his brothers, too. I see it, black in my veins as I sit reluctantly in the doctor's office; I hear it, heavy in my voice as I struggle to *integrate*.

As Ceija Stojka wrote, "ich lebe mit meinen verstorbenen" - *I live with my deceased*. It was not the encounter with death that brought the most pain but the ongoing experience of having survived it. Maami's half-told stories carried the weight of her family members as though she carried their bones directly. Perhaps she did, perhaps that's what these words, these silences are - the remains of her family, their silhouettes shrouded in *hungry smoke*.

And as children we carry them too. We may not know their names or their faces, but we feel the weight of their absences. We hear the breaking of hearts as they're poured into whisky glasses. Their emptiness crawls into the corner of our eyes as we watch the future unfold without them. As we walk through our lives, we walk with our hungry ghosts - those left behind, always looking for the leaves on the road and the woodsmoke in the distance.

ENDNOTES

[1] Germany finally commemorates Roma victims of Holocaust, Alexandra Hudson, Reuters, 10/23/2012

[2] Popular Trauma Culture, Anne Rothe, Rutgers University Press, 2011

[3] Sociology Confronts the Holocaust: Memories and Identities in Jewish Diasporas, Judith Gerson and Diane Wolf, Duke University Press, 2007

[4] The Nazi Persecution of the Gypsies, Guenter Lewy, Oxford University Press, 2000

[5] The Nazi Genocide of the Roma: Reassessment and Commemoration, Anton Weiss-Wendt, Berghahn Books, 2013

[6] Negotiating the 'state of exception': Gypsies' encounter with the judiciary in Germany and Italy 1860-1914, Jennifer Illuzzi, Routledge, 2010

[7] "To be or not to be" Sinti, Gypsy, and Romani: Crisis of Sinti ethnic identity, Rinaldo diRicchardi-Reinhardt, 2014

[8] Nous, on n'en parle pas: les vivants et les morts chez le Manouches, Patrick Williams, Editions de la Maison des sciences de l'homme, 1993

[9] To be or not to be" Sinti, Gypsy, and Romani: Crisis of Sinti ethnic identity, Rinaldo diRicchardi-Reinhardt, 2014

[10] Intent, Failure of Plans, and Escalation: Nazi Persecution of the Gypsies in Germany and Austria, 1933-1942, Michael Zimmerman, US Holocaust Memorial Museum Symposium Proceedings, Roma and Sinti Under-studied Victims of Nazism, 2002

[11] "To be or not to be" Sinti, Gypsy, and Romani: Crisis of Sinti ethnic identity, Rinaldo diRicchardi-Reinhardt, 2014

[12] Leg dich, Zigeuner. Die Gesichter von Johann Trollmann und Tull Harder, Roger Repplinger, Piper, 2012

[13] Leg dich, Zigeuner. Die Gesichter von Johann Trollmann und Tull Harder, Roger Repplinger, Piper, 2012

[14] 1924: The Year That Made Hitler, Peter Ross Range, Little, Brown and Company, 2015

[15] Bareknuckle: Memoirs of the Undefeated Champion, Bartley Gorman, The Overlook Press, 2011

[16] When Boxing was, like, Ridiculously Racist, Ian Carey, 2013
[17] On Boxing, Joyce Carol Oates, Harper, 2006
[18] Hitlerland: American Witnesses to the Nazi Rise to Power, Andrew Nagorski, Simon and Schuster, 2013
[19] When Boxing Was A Jewish Sport, Alan Bodner, Praeger Publishers, 1997
[20] Django: the Life and Music of a Gypsy Legend, Michael Dregni, Oxford University Press, 2004
[21] Bareknuckle: Memoirs of the Undefeated Champion, Bartley Gorman, The Overlook Press, 2011
[22] http://www.stuff.co.nz/sport/other-sports/74535333/born-to-box-factbox-on-new-world-heavyweight-champion-tyson-fury
[23] Leg dich, Zigeuner. Die Gesichter von Johann Trollmann und Tull Harder, Roger Repplinger, Piper, 2012
[24] Hiterland: American Witnesses to the Nazi Rise to Power, Andrew Nagorski, Simon and Schuster, 2013
[25] Der Boxer, Felix Mitterer, Haymon-Taschenbuch, 2015
[26] The Nazi Persecution of the Gypsies, Guenter Lewy (see above reference)
[27] The Nazi Persecution of the Gypsies, Guenter Lewy (see above reference)
[28] Got Fight? The 50 en Principles of Hand-to-Face Combat, Forrest Griffin, William Morrow, 2010
[29] On Boxing, Joyce Carol Oates (see above reference)
[30] Jack Sharkey: A Heavyweight Champion's Untold Story, James Curl, Win By KO Publications, 2015
[31] Life in the Third Reich, Daily Life in Nazi Germany 1933-1945, Paul Roland, Arcturus Publishing
[32] Hitlerland: American Witnesses to the Nazi Rise to Power, Andrew Nagorski, Simon and Schuster, 2013
[33] 1924: The Year That Made Hitler, Peter Ross Range, Little, Brown and Company, 2015
[34] Hitler's Olympics: The Story of the 196 Nazi Games, Anton Rippon, Pen and Sword, 2012
[35] Hitlerland: American Witnesses to the Nazi Rise to Power, Andrew Nagorski, Simon and Schuster, 2013

[36] The Roma Struggle for Compensation in Post-War Germany, Julia von dem Knesebeck, University of Hertfordshire Press, 2011
[37] Foiled: Hitler's Jewish Olympian: The Helene Mayer Story, Milly Mogulof, RDR Books, 2001
[38] Hitlerland: American Witnesses to the Nazi Rise to Power, Andrew Nagorski, Simon and Schuster, 2013
[39] Hitler's Olympics: The Story of the 196 Nazi Games, Anton Rippon, Pen and Sword, 2012
[40] The Maisky Diaries: Red Ambassador to the Court of Saint James, Ivan Maiskey, Gabriel Gorodetsky, Yale University Press, 2015
[41] Der Boxer, Felix Mitterer, Haymon-Taschenbuch, 2015
[42] Up in smoke goes the lie that the Holocaust was a big secret, The Higher Education Times, Lisa Pine, May 2006
[43] Crossing, Jan Yoors, Simon and Schuster, 1971
[44] Oral interview with Kore Yoors
[45] Crossing, Jan Yoors, Simon and Schuster, 1971
[46] The Nazi Genocide of the Roma: Reassessment and Commemoration, Anton Weiss-Wendt (see above reference)
[47] The Nazi Persecution of the Gypsies, Lewy (see above reference)
[48] The German Opposition to Hitler, Michael Thomsett, Cruz Publishers (to be published)
[49] The truth behind the French Resistance Myth, Nicholas Shakespeare, The Telegraph, 9/4/2015
[50] Leg dich, Zigeuner. Die Gesichter von Johann Trollmann und Tull Harder, Roger Repplinger, Piper, 2012
[51] Leg dich, Zigeuner. Die Gesichter von Johann Trollmann (see above reference)
[52] Dietrich & Riefenstahl: Hollywood, Berlin, and a Century in Two Lives, Karin Wieland, Liveright, 2015
[53] Gypsy Sexuality: Romani and Outsider Perspectives on Intimacy, Nirenberg, Clambake Press, 2011
[54] Oral interview; subject chooses anonymity
[55] Leg dich, Zigeuner. Die Gesichter von Johann Trollmann und Tull Harder, Roger Repplinger, Piper, 2012
[56] Life in the Third Reich, Daily Life in Nazi Germany 1933-1945, Paul Roland

[57] http://2august.eu/the-roma-genocide/16-may-romani-resistence-day/
[58] The Nazi Persecution of the Gypsies, Guenter Lewy (see above reference)
[59] The Nazi Genocide of the Roma: Reassessment and Commemoration, Anton Weiss-Wendt, 2013
[60] The Nazi Genocide of the Roma: Reassessment and Commemoration, Anton Weiss-Wendt, 2013
[61] Tragedia Romilor Deportati in Transnistria 1942-1945, Radu Ioanid, Michelle Kelso and Lumunita Cioaba, Editura Polirom, 2009
[62] Romanian Romani Resistance to Genocide in the Matrix of the Tigan Other, Anthropology of East Europe Review, Shannon Woodcock, 2008
[63] The Holocaust in Romania: The Destruction of the Jews and Gypsies Under the Antonescu Regime 1940-44, Radu Ioanid, Ivan R. Dee, 2008
[64] Tragedia Romilor Deportati in Transnistria 1942-1945, Radu Ioanid, Michelle Kelso and Lumunita Cioaba
[65] The Holocaust in Romania: The Destruction of Jews and Gypsies Under the Antonescu Regime 1940-44, Radu Ioanid, Ivan R. Dee, 2008
[66] The Holocaust in Romania: The Destruction of Jews and Gypsies Under the Antonescu Regime 1940-44, Radu Ioanid, Ivan R. Dee, 2008
[67] Leg dich. Zigeuner. Die Gesichter von Johann Trollmann und Tull Harder, Roger Repplinger, Piper, 2012
[68] The Boxer: the True Story of Holocaust Survivor Harry Haft, Reinhard Kleist, Self Made Hero, 2014
[69] Leg dich, Zigeuner. Die Gesichter von Johann Trollmann und Tull Harder, Roger Repplinger, Piper, 2012
[70] Crossing, Jan Yoors (see above reference)
[71] Elie Wiesel, Simon Wiesenthal, Romanies and the U.S. Holocaust Memorial Council, The Holocaust in History and Memory, Ian Hancock (2011)
[72] The Final Chapter, Donald Kenrick University of Hertfordshire Press, 2006
[73] The Final Chapter, Donald Kenrick (see above reference)

[74] The Nazi Persecution of the Gypsies, Guenter Lewy (see above reference)
[75] The Nazi Genocide of the Roma: Reassessment and Commemoration, Anton Weiss-Wendt, 2013
[76] Handwritten note attached to copy of death record, US Holocaust Memorial Museum archive
[77] Gypsy Protesters Driven From a Nazi Camp, Sergey Schmemann, New York Times, 10/4, 1989
[78] The Nazi Genocide of the Roma: Reassessment and Commemoration, Anton Weiss-Wendt, 2013
[79] The Nazi Persecution of the Gypsies, Guenter Lewy (see above reference)
[80] The Roma Struggle for Compensation in Post-War Germany, Julia von dem Knesebeck (see above reference)
[81] Life in the Third Reich: Daily Life in Nazi Germany 1933-1945, Paul Roland
[82] John Le Carre, the Biography, Adam Sisman, Harper, 2015
[83] The Roma Struggle for Compensation in Post-War Germany, Julia von dem Knesebeck, University of Hertfordshire Press, 2011
[84] The Roma Struggle for Compensation in Post-War Germany, Julia von dem Knesebeck, University of Hertfordshire Press, 2011
[85] The Roma Struggle for Compensation in Post-War Germany, Julia von dem Knesebeck (see above reference)
[86] The Holocaust in Romania: The Destruction of Jews and Gypsies Under the Antonescu Regime 1940-44, Radu Ioanid, Ivan R. Dee, 2008
[87] Two Decades After the Wall's Fall: End of Communism Cheered but Now with More Reservations, The Pew Global Attitudes Project, 2009
[88] Nous, on n'en parle pas: les vivants et les morts chez le Manouches, Patrick Williams, Editions de la Maison des sciences de l'homme, 1993
[89] Popular Trauma Culture, Anne Rothe, Rutgers University Press, 2011
[90] Ally: My Journey Across the American-Israeli Divide, Michael Oren, Random House, 2015

[91] http://www.errc.org/blog/the-world-has-learned-nothing-from-the-holocaust%E2%80%A6/72
[92] The Nazi Genocide of the Roma: Reassessment and Commemoration, Anton Weiss-Wendt, 2013
[93] The Roma Holocaust Memorial That Wasn't Built in a Day, Ofer Aderet, Haaretz, 9/14/2012
[94] "I can say that because I am a Jew. They don't care about the Sinti and Roma.", Ruth Schneider, ExBerliner, 1/10/2013
[95] Responses to the Porrajmos (The Romani Holocaust), Is the Holocaust Unique?, Ian Hancock, The Westview Press, 1995
[96] Responses to the Porrajmos (The Romani Holocaust), Is the Holocaust Unique?, Ian Hancock, The Westview Press, 1995
[97] Elie Wiesel, Simon Wiesenthal, Romanies and the U.S. Holocaust Memorial Council, The Holocaust in History and Memory, Ian Hancock, 2011
[98] Elie Wiesel, Simon Wiesenthal, Romanies and the U.S. Holocaust Memorial Council, The Holocaust in History and Memory, Ian Hancock (2011)
[99] http://www.advarsitysports.com/andrea-pirlo-and-its-origins-no-sinti-but-only-a-gypsy-of-the-midfield/
[100] http://www.wired.co.uk/news/archive/2014-06/18/hatebrain-stats-uk

Lightning Source UK Ltd.
Milton Keynes UK
UKHW041248211021
392594UK00001B/139